Applying the Lessons of
UK NATIONAL
POLITICS
to Everyday Office Life

This book is dedicated to
my mother and sister

Applying the Lessons of
UK NATIONAL
POLITICS
to Everyday Office Life

LEARNING FROM CABINET MINISTERS AND MPs

RICHARD WILLIS

sussex
ACADEMIC
PRESS
Brighton • Chicago • Toronto

2 4 6 8 10 9 7 5 3 1

First published in 2019 by
SUSSEX ACADEMIC PRESS
PO Box 139
Eastbourne BN24 9BP

Distributed in North America by
SUSSEX ACADEMIC PRESS
Independent Publishers Group
814 N. Franklin Street, Chicago, IL 60610

British Library Cataloguing in Publication Data
A CIP catalogue record for this book is available from the British Library.

Library of Congress Cataloging-in-Publication Data
Applied for.

Paperback ISBN 978-1-84519-988-3

Typeset and designed by Sussex Academic Press, Brighton & Eastbourne.
Printed by TJ International, Padstow, Cornwall.

Contents

Acknowledgements

The cover illustrations for print and electronic usage are reproduced by permission of 123RF GB Ltd (London).

The photographers: Adrian Hillman (office workers; stock number: 9565798); Aberbran Studio (10 Downing St: stock number: 55161730); Vichaya Kiatying-Angsulee (Parliament: stock number: 13405680).

Introduction

This book takes an enterprising approach to our knowledge of office politics in that it is based on findings from interviews of two former Cabinet Ministers and a survey of UK MPs. The essential purpose of these investigative tools is to give an account of the 'politicking' of government in the British political system and the ways in which these findings have a bearing on office politics, a process to which so many of us are subject in our daily lives. The intention is to arm the office worker with defensive and offensive tactics in order to establish themselves in the life of the office. I show that, while a more conciliatory and democratic approach is feasible, built on goodwill, helpfulness and humanitarian values, it may be less effective.

In the background is always the British welfare state, founded after the Second World War. Housing rented from the state, the National Health Service, social security, free education and many other elements were brought in to prevent a revolution by the working classes – the welfare state was seen a way to avoid a civil war, but the aim was also to reward the citizens of Britain for all the losses and sacrifices made during the war. It is necessary still to take on board both perspectives.

Office politics may be defined here as actions, attitudes, opinions, strategies and behaviour geared to promoting oneself ahead of other workers in the workplace. An alternative is the practice of democratic ideals and motives to instil a sense of fair play and harmony in accomplishing one's career aims. Within the office it is clear that the employer can have a soft voice but carry a big stick.

Qualifications and Experience

My experience of offices consists of ten years' employment in the law department of a US multi-national, which held ten qualified barristers and solicitors, two legal assistants, four secretaries and an office manager. My duties were to run the law library, to administer the lawyers' continuing professional development in accordance with Law Society regulations, to report monthly to Houston in the USA on lawyers' outside counsel fees, and other associated tasks. I also worked in central London, including the City, for a year, and in financial administration at a London teaching hospital for 18 months. I have worked in administration for the Cambridge University Press, the TEC National Council, the Bank of Scotland, The Civil Service, the Battersea Bedsit Project, Battersea Technical College, the Probation Service and the London Borough of Lambeth. I would hope that these experiences have added to my ability to examine and discuss some of the essentials of office politics and the actions of those in the workplace.

Much of the inspiration for and interest in this book comes from the acclaimed academic and civil servant Maurice Kogan. He was my tutor, friend and mentor while he was Professor of Government and Social Administration at Brunel University, a post he held for more than 25 years before an outstanding contribution in the Civil Service. While reading political science, I elected, in the final year, to do Kogan's module on politics and policy-making. As an undergraduate, I met Shirley Williams, Ken Livingstone, Sir Keith Joseph, Jim Callaghan, Dr David Owen, Cecil Parkinson and Professor Tony Travers. Kogan was particularly expert on the politics of education as evidenced by his publication recording conversations with Edward Boyle and Anthony Crosland (both former Education Ministers).[1] I consciously used the model employed by Kogan in his interviews and asked questions similar to those posed by Kogan in his analysis.

---

1   M. Kogan, *The Politics of Education*, London: Penguin, 1974.

My interest in contemporary politics was initiated when I became an advisor to David Cameron's team reviewing the public services when the Conservative party was in opposition. My services were called upon largely as a result of my work in teacher education, including 11 years as a senior researcher based at Roehampton University, as an advisor to the Qualifications and Curriculum Development Authority and as the author of *The Struggle for the General Teaching Council*.[2] I presented my thoughts and observations on the teaching profession in Parliament to Stephen Dorell, Health Secretary under John Major, and Baroness Pauline Perry. We considered proposals intended to raise the profession's importance, to counter poor professional standards in the past and to modernise and reform Britain's education services. I also interviewed Charlotte Leslie MP about her role in supporting institutional reform, such as the setting up of the Chartered College of Teaching in January 2017.

Oral Testimony

My exposure to oral testimony was reinforced when I was a research associate at Cambridge University for a history project funded by the Leverhulme Trust where, working with two dons and two senior researchers, I contributed to the interviewing of over 100 former teachers. The study shed much new light on how practical and professional goals were questioned within the broader national and local policy objectives for teacher training.[3] We found that teaching offered an upwardly mobile path from the working classes to the middle class.[4] The eventual publication coming from this project led Ted Wragg, the British academic and author, to comment in the *Times Educational Supplement* that our study 'shows how oral history should be done'.[5]

---

2   R. Willis, *The Struggle for the General Teaching Council*, London and New York: Routledge/Falmer, 2005.

3   P. Cunningham and P. Gardner, *Becoming Teachers, Texts and Testimonies 1907–1950*, London: Woburn Press, 2004.

4   R. Willis, 'Learning in the Classroom', *History Today*, April 2007, pp. 39–40.

5   T. Wragg, 'Book of the Week, Trainees tell it like it was', *Times Educational Supplement*, 19 December 2003, p. 29.

Oral testimony, of the kind given in the Appendix to this book by Lord (Kenneth) Baker and Lord (David) Blunkett, allows the reader to learn more about the perspectives of individuals, information that might not otherwise appear in historical records. Oral history also provides a great opportunity to interact with others, and researchers and interviewees join together in conversation about a shared interest, something that can be very rewarding both for those interviewing and those being interviewed. Efforts were made to provide due weight to political affiliation, experience and the extent to which policies have impacted on politics since the end of the Second World War. I anticipated that the two former Cabinet ministers selected for the exercise could testify to particular aspects of decision-making and power in government that would be relevant to building on and increasing our knowledge of office politics. The interviewees offered a rich source of data and this was supplemented with material from written publications, including diaries and memoirs. The survey that I draw on in this book provided important data about MPs who were or had been engaged in the political process and who were able to comment on their own office and administrative experience. The outcome was a vast amount of information that could be applied to an analysis of office politics. The names of surveyed MPs are not revealed as at the outset it was agreed that they would remain anonymous. It was felt that in this way the MP could be more honest and would not be castigated if they had not followed the party line.

The interviews were structured, and I asked a series of questions to each politician who replied in the way they saw fit and so the interaction assisted me to gain some valuable insights derived straight from those actively employed in politics.

How the Book is Organised

I start by setting out some background; including the careers of the two interviewees whose views have contributed so much to informing the Parliamentary political analysis in this book. I go on to examine limitations on power in politics (in government and in the office), present examples of various ways in which power might be exercised (drawing parallels between 'headline' politics and events in workplaces) and look specifically at change and reform in government and in the office. Lastly, I include a short case study, looking at the John Lewis Organisation. The full interviews of Lord Baker and Lord Blunkett are given as an Appendix.

1

Elective Dictatorship

Government is constrained by a set of checks and balances, to protect individual liberties and supposedly to limit overzealous and tyrannical rulers. The office is a microcosm of this particular activity.

Although accusations of elective dictatorial rule were made against Margaret Thatcher and Tony Blair, both could lay claim to substantial majorities in Parliament and therefore to a clear mandate to govern. Yet despite a wave of public outcry opposing the invasion of Iraq in 2003, Blair acted in concert with President Bush and chose to ignore the body of public opinion against going to war, and this certainly imperilled the future of his government. It is interesting to note, as an aside, that Peter Ustinov's delivery when playing Emperor Nero in the film *Quo Vadis* resembled the tone adopted by Blair when he spoke outside 10 Downing Street at the moment New Labour won its first election victory.

Like the mandate a British government receives from its electorate, management can gain the consent of its employees to be managed – and lose it. In applying the concepts of political science to office politics, my intention is to examine the role of ministers and how we may view ourselves as stakeholders in the office, acting in a way that will further our aims and ambitions. Examining the political purpose of the various branches of government may help us look at our careers and see more clearly the vital ingredients to bring about change in our own lives. In a democracy, there are many competing forces at work in making policy and this study is designed to identify what these stimuli are, how they affect the minister/management, and the extent to which we, as office personnel, can pick up tips and tactics to aid ourselves in the work we aspire to or already do. I review the extent to which governments and organisations can appear impervious to pressures from outside while carrying through their policies, in spite of internal and external forces trying to influence their views.

In Parliament, at Question Time, no love is lost between the political parties present. The bitterness of the House of Commons exchanges is vitriolic, and the MPs can be very hostile and aggressive towards each other. A clash of personalities, with all their faults and disorders, can exasperate the degree of conflict exhibited. Learn what lessons you can from these debates and observe how during their work MPs defend themselves, and their civil servants. This can be of use when you are challenged either by your boss, your colleagues or others from outside the organisation who might set about giving you a hard time. Where you can access a TV, notice the way in which the prime minister defends the government's policies, using a wide vocabulary and turn of speech that command respect. In other cases deference might be a good policy, but avoid advantage being taken of you and try to stand up for yourself where the occasion demands. This is of key importance where other staff or management are rude or disrespectful to you. When MPs are interviewed by the media, if they find the interviewer over-assertive, they might reply 'With respect, you have asked me a question; let me answer it'.

This study questions and records the knowledge of politicians whose views can help cast light on the nature of administrative processes and procedures and can be stored to serve as an enduring legacy to their experiences in office settings.

The Changing Life of the Political Economy and the Office

The terms in office of my main interviewees (the Rt Hon. Kenneth, Lord Baker and the Rt Hon. David, Lord Blunkett) saw questions raised about the integrity of democratic rule; where the various tranches of management claim a mandate to act, that mandate may be questioned by those tasked with carrying out the action. The dominance of the executive is something that the two main political parties embody in their ideological perceptions of the British constitution. The Conservatives view authority as flowing from above and they prefer independent government, with the public reduced to voting every five years or whenever there is a general election (such as Theresa May's decision to call a snap election in 2017). The Conservatives have traditionally shied away from reform but in recent years they have displayed much enthusiasm for improving the lot of the private individual. They praise the loyalty of their local supporters and claim that, once a government has a mandate to govern, firm leadership should be assumed and directed to establishing a strong hold on the political affairs of the nation. If this view is applied to offices, they can be seen as theatres of political intrigue and there are arguments that the ideal way to manage is to get the backing and cooperation of the staff, so that each member acquires a sense of identity and the perception that they have a purpose within the workplace. Nonetheless (in this view), the freedoms of each member of staff must be curtailed, since there is a need for firm governance and a manager must show determination to lead from the front where appropriate.

The Labour party has also supported the concept of a strong executive but favours the predominance of the principle of Parliamentary representation for the working class, though New Labour depended crucially on support from the middle classes in gaining electoral success. Labour governments have encouraged social mobility for the lower classes; but this segment of society has become less relevant to the cause of socialism and entertained desires to protect and enhance their economic welfare, which has been improved by several administrations since the Second

World War. (The Conservatives have been equally assiduous, offering the working classes such benefits as home ownership through the chance to buy social housing.) Traditionally the trade unions have sought to achieve working-class solidarity, but the influence of left-wing policies, such as those advocated by Tony Benn, and more recently by Jeremy Corbyn, has dwindled. Programmes of reform have propelled the party forward and it has been committed to protecting the rights of the individual against institutional forces posing a threat to freedoms, and from overbearing leaderships.

The desire for reform is also expressed by the Liberals or Liberal Democrats. Their activism in favour of Parliamentary reform in the nineteenth century is a case in point. In more recent times, the Liberal Party campaigned for entry to the European Economic Community and measures to bring formal devolution remain at the centre of their policies. The mantle for reform was taken up by Deputy Prime Minister Nick Clegg when joining the Coalition Government in 2010: he promised a major overhaul of British democracy, changes as radical as the Great Reform Act of 1832. Radical reforms were also sought by the UK Independence Party led by Nigel Farage (UKIP), favouring the departure from Europe (or 'Brexit', as it is now known).

The turning point occurred in the mid-1970s at a time when economic and social strife set in. The very foundations of the British economy changed: a job for life and the ability to find work without much hassle became phenomena of the past. In the 1960s employment could be easily found and freedoms were spread as widely as they have ever been. The coming of the Beatles, the sexual revolution and the heyday of the hippie brought with them a new way of living as Britain emerged once and for all from the constraints of the Second World War and Austerity (Fifties-style). In these times the debate began to threaten the core of constitutional precedent and procedure, both in the office and in national politics. The possibility of social advancement brought with it demands for greater professional opportunity and so political infighting, gossip, and pressure to maintain one's position within the organisation, ambition, bitching, manipulating, sucking up and diverting blame. In central government deep-seated questions were raised, albeit on the surface a less ruthless agenda, about the value of ministerial responsibility, the efficacy of cabinet government, the desirability of continuing with the electoral system, and concerns about Parliamentary rule. Such issues, while perhaps undergoing a lull in the 1960s, continued to rage on.

Changes to the constitution accelerated after 1997 following the Labour Government victory that year. That government removed most of the hereditary peers from the House of Lords, passed the Human Rights Act 1998, set up devolved governments in Scotland, Wales and the English regions and signed a peace accord in Northern Ireland. These reforms were accompanied by the introduction of proportional representation for the devolved parliaments in the UK, the European parliament and the London Assembly. Much of the new legislation was radical, and a Scottish referendum was even held to ask whether that nation should remain in the UK; the result, an overwhelming vote to stay in the UK has seen constitutional activists relegated to the sidelines.

Political skullduggery has perhaps changed its methods since the 1960s. The divisions in the Cabinet over Brexit challenge completely the doctrine of collective responsibility and the law that 'we'd better all be in the same story'. Regarding Britain's membership of the European Union and Brexit, now an issue at the centre of British politics, a new set of questions are asked. The European Communities Act of 1972 allows EC law occasionally to override legislation approved by Parliament, and more commonly forces Parliament to take action. Such a development was anathema to a large section of the British public and UKIP capitalised on this feeling of disapproval, being at that time united in its wish to see the UK withdraw from the EU. In January 2013 the Prime Minister David Cameron promised a referendum on British membership of the EU if the Conservative party gained a majority at the next general election. A major concern was that decisions made in Europe were having an adverse impact on the outcome of political events in the UK. Some argued that the sovereignty of Parliament had been put in jeopardy and others claimed that the Eurosceptics and those in UKIP used the EU as a scapegoat for Britain's own political, social and economic ills. Hostility towards the EU was particularly present among the working classes in some marginal constituencies and UKIP built a strong power base in those constituencies, but although support was spread across the nation it was not concentrated enough to translate into seats. The populist vote was success-fully harnessed, the referendum drew a majority for leaving the EU and Cameron resigned.

The British Constitution and the Office

Traditionally, the British constitution has owed much to stabil-ity and cohesion, relying on a sound political order formalised by the spread of civil society and growth in the economy since the eighteenth century. Britain has prided itself on combining within its constitution a historical tradition built up over cen-turies, with democracy and strong government. Upheavals and crises still occur but rarely. Since the 1970s, recurring reces-sions and the 2008 Crash, membership of the European Union, Brexit and the calls for greater devolution within the UK, have all called into question the effectiveness of the British constitution.

Office workers have gained protections through laws preventing discrimination and prejudice. The laws against discrimination have opened doors, allowing, for example, for a personal assis-tant to provide an administrative service to an advocate who was blind and who took on cases to counter unfair dismissal in the workplace (Mandy Maddocks). These protections have partic-ularly been in the areas of equality and disability, for example the various measures over thirty years or so that were consoli-dated in the Equality Act 2010. In 2019, it is widely perceived that we have been seeing only the tip of the 'iceberg' of those suffering from mental illness. Claims of one sufferer in every four of the population, or even one in three, have been bandied about, and members of the Royal Family – Princes William and Harry – have shared their own problems, encouraging more and more disabled people to come out and admit to being victims of mental illness. Government actions are increasingly being directed to this policy priority and more money is being pumped in to help the mentally ill. The work here is long overdue and there is still much prejudice to overcome. Iain Duncan Smith MP, when in government, introduced changes to save social security costs, which make it harder for the sick to claim benefits, and these have not helped. Tragic cases have emerged, including suicides and other deaths. It must be admitted that the changes have seen a crackdown on unjustified and even fraudulent claims, which is a positive step forward and one that partly explains recent increases in employment, but this development comes with a cost to genuine benefit seekers, which is widely seen as unfair and poorly thought-through. Parallels have been drawn with Spain during the 2008 Crash, when governments withheld funding for the needy poor, causing many to take their own lives in despair.

Where offices have found themselves unable to adapt to changing circumstances and events then political legitimacy has sprung up informally to regulate office politicking through conventions and practices that gain acceptance as the way in which office staff should be managed. Where respectability has been achieved, lessons learned following the British template have gained international credence and acclaim; flexibility, instilled by democracy and effective management, has become a notable feature of office behaviour. Certain organisations, particularly charities, show less evidence of office politics, but to say that it is absent in any group setting is wrong (and silly). One senior executive, among his trappings of power, would frequently seek to check a person's behaviour by pointing out that their actions conflicted with norms and how a person ought to behave. Thus, if an individual persistently talked about football, they would be admonished by this manager for doing so. The manager would intervene like this when he felt threatened – he had hardly any interest in sport and would deal with his lack of knowledge by pulling up his subordinate in this way.

Since the 1970s, the concept of a job for life has virtually disappeared. With the disappearance of career security has come fears of mergers between companies and of over-centralisation of government, and these have persisted in the press. The inadequacy of checks on managerial and government authority has come to dominate some debates, as well as concerns about uncertainty, the existence of an 'elective dictatorship', unscrupulous bosses and exploitation, and a recent decline in the protection of rights. The looseness of the rules at the heart of office practice and of government, such as the meaning of the doctrine of individual ministerial responsibility, has been questioned. For example, should Ministers resign even where a minor civil servant has made a mistake?

Job security for many occupational groups is tenuous and when unemployment is high the going can be rough, though some managers, MPs, and staff can still retain their jobs for long periods. MPs can rely on additional lucrative employment outside Parliament which can help them financially, not only while in the House of Commons but also when they retire or lose their seat. They are often Oxbridge graduates, and were previously solicitors or barristers and/or go on to well-paid directorships.

When an office employee is 'let go', they will be looking for references and well-presented CVs to gain alternative employment elsewhere. Office qualifications and experience are important, marketable and transferable skills to have. Office personnel can get professional qualifications, for example a Higher National in business and finance or a vocational level 3 or 4 in business and administration. Those wanting to become a manager or director might go for level 4 or a degree in business. A knowledge of Microsoft Office, especially Word and Excel, can virtually always lead to work, whether temporary or permanent and such employment can always keep the wolf from the door. Despite the many frailties of 'the market economy', where there is evidence of long employment, unembellished and with few setbacks, this can enhance the prospect of finding a new job. Like Theresa May, who became leader of the Conservatives in

an initial wave of enthusiasm after the fiasco of the Brexit referendum, office personnel can benefit from a change of
management. In the world of politics, fresh faces in the premiership, such as in recent times Margaret Thatcher, John Major,
Tony Blair, Gordon Brown, David Cameron and Theresa May,
have all enjoyed a 'honeymoon' period in government, some for
longer than others. Admin staff never achieve the meteoric levels
of pay or perks that ministers can (especially prime ministers),
but a PA or top executive assistant can secure a good standard of
living and can earn well above national average earnings, as much
as £50,000 in London.

Politics and Principles

As a politician the name of the game is taking criticism on the
chin and there is not always a real possibility of appealing to a
higher person or body to seek redress. Having been given the
opportunity to score a few points against their opponents, few
MPs say no to putting their opponents down. David Blunkett, in
his interview, could not resist a crack at his successor Michael
Gove's policies: 'It's hard to believe that improved standards in
the classroom, which is at the very heart of any improvement in
education, can be validated by believing that you could have
untrained teachers in the classroom . . . It's hard to believe that
you want extraordinarily good, world-class leadership if you're
able to bring people in as school leaders who've got no experience
of school leadership.' MPs can seek solace among those who
share their political beliefs, but in the main they are open to attack
not just from their opponents in other parties, but also from the
press. While, at Westminster, it is good that we have a system
such as this in order to keep tabs on politicians, office politicians
would do well to take heed of this potential to attract bullying and
verbal abuse.

Another area that the office manager should be aware of, which
has parallels in government, is the fall-out if members (of staff;
of government) are involved with shady or underhand activity.
The Labour MP Keith Vaz resigned as chairman of the influen-

tial Home Affairs select committee after allegations emerged that he had paid for sex with male prostitutes. The MP's public image is always under scrutiny: they occupy a position where there are expected to follow a scandal-free life, but sadly that they do go astray is all too often a feature of political life. While office workers' private lives are not as open to scrutiny as those of MPs, every office has standards and behaviour that it expects to be followed.

MPs, one would like to think, are influenced by political philosophy, and many have studied the subject at university. You could take a page out of their book and be motivated to read, say, the classic political philosophers and economists such as Jean-Jacques Rousseau or Adam Smith. Reading such texts and commentaries, you can pick up tactics which can feed through to office politics. Rousseau's theory of the general will, for example, can provide you with honourable motives for office behaviour. The idea is that when you act you do so more because there is a general consensus that this is what is required than necessarily because it directly favours your own ends. The path you take, however, may depend on circumstances. You might wish to lead a moral life, and regard Rousseau's amorality as unacceptable, but if you are the office scapegoat then there is a strong case for you to take Rousseau's line. But there are others. You might find more profit from reading the works of Adam Smith, who held among other things that the pursuit of self-interest underlies the economy.

The study of political philosophy, much aided David Blunkett, who saw his three years at university as contributing to his political persona. He was given an opportunity to examine competing political theories and their application in the modern era. He admits that the common good can be underpinned by enlightened self-interest, a statement you would not necessarily expect from a Labour supporter. So, it may be necessary to go with the flow, and deviate when necessary to form new partnerships or alliances, to do away with what you see as lesser strategies and to employ new tactics in a way that will help you to rise above the frictions and battles that can mar your working days. If you were trying to protect your child, you would persuade people to look after them and might instinctively take the actions necessary to prevent harm to them, no matter what laws you broke or what underhand measures you were forced to adopt.

The freedoms exercised by Kenneth Baker and David Blunkett in government have led to much debate on whether too much power is concentrated at the centre of government. Hierarchies in the office, albeit on a smaller stage, suggest that within an informal setting individuals of the same administrative grade exercise greater power than their colleagues. The role of equality here has been given much importance and some say it is key to thinking on the current political agenda. In reality the notion of equality in a socialist context is really a chimera and geared towards a utopia which is impossible to attain. George Orwell explained that in society there are three levels, high, medium and low. Power is invested in any of these strata and from time to time it may shift from one grouping to another. In his acclaimed book *Nineteen Eighty-Four*, Orwell writes:

> The aims of these three groups are entirely irreconcilable. The aim of the High is to remain where they are. The aim of the Middle is to change places with the High. The aim of the Low, when they have an aim – for it is an abiding characteristic of the Low that they are too much crushed by drudgery to be more than intermittently conscious of anything outside their daily lives – is to abolish all distinctions and create a society in which all men shall be equal.[6]

---

6 G. Orwell, *Nineteen Eighty-Four*, London: Penguin, 1987 (original, 1948).

2

Interviews:
Lord Baker
and Lord Blunkett

Here is some background on the two leading candidates whom I interviewed.

The Rt Hon. the Lord Baker of Dorking

Kenneth Baker (Baron Baker of Dorking) was a Cabinet Minister in Margaret Thatcher's government, being the architect of some of its most controversial policies. He was Party Chairman and spent seven years in the Cabinet.

He underwent his National Service as an army lieutenant, and was employed by Royal Dutch Shell before being elected as a Member of Parliament at a by-election in 1968. He was appointed Minister of Information Technology in 1981 and four years later became Secretary of State for the Environment. He served as Secretary of State for Education between 1986 and 1989. He was later promoted to Home Secretary.

During Lord Baker's time as Secretary for Education, he introduced the National Curriculum in the 1988 Education Act and wound up the University Grants Committee, replacing it with the short-lived Universities Funding Council. This book gives a focus on these fields, including advice on how best to work in the office on the basis of knowledge gained from the interviews I conducted with Ken Baker.

What with the very high number of young people going to university and gaining a degree, the prospect of finding an office job is becoming more and more common. Some graduates, particularly those who have studied politics or history, can be very keen to take up employment in which they can apply the lessons they have learnt in higher education. The ability to transfer skills and knowledge from degree courses is now very necessary in the commercial world. Ken Baker had wanted a career in business, as was evident from his early job at Shell. In 1968 he decided that he wanted to become an MP. Working in an office may not seem glamorous, but if you are ambitious you have every possibility to gain promotion and if not you may find your level and settle with that. Baker made his choice and decided to enter politics. The norm for potential Conservative MPs then was to fight (and most probably fail to win) a safe Labour seat (Poplar in his case), then fight a marginal (Acton, which he won in 1968), and then a strongly held Conservative seat (Marylebone in 1970, and ten years later Mole Valley, till his retirement in 1997).

Baker's father had wanted him to be a civil servant. Baker did not find that attractive. His father was a little upset. Baker's choice involved ultimately working alongside civil servants, so he did not deviate too far from his father's expectations.

Apparently, Margaret Thatcher gave Baker a fairly wide brief. In 1986 she called him in and told him to go away and come back to her in two months, at the end of which he could tell her more about his ideas in education. With the pressure lifted, he was able to work out his policies for the Education Reform Act of 1988. A message here for the office manager: you might do well to lift the strain on your staff, by allowing them time to perform their duties.

The Rt Hon. the Lord Blunkett

David Blunkett experienced many setbacks early in his life: the death of his father, a Gas Board foreman, in an accident at work when he was 12 years old, poverty and his experiences as a blind child: his education was exclusive rather than inclusive. All these disadvantages made a difference to his perspective and he wanted 'to change the world for the better'.

A disciplined and conscientious individual, he excelled academically and professionally, becoming a Labour councillor while studying at Sheffield University. In June 1980 he was elected to the post of Leader of Sheffield City Council. In June 1987 he took up a seat in Parliament as Labour MP for Sheffield Brightside. After New Labour's landslide victory in 1997 he was appointed Secretary of State for Education and Employment and after further electoral success in 2001, Blunkett became Home Secretary.

This study considers David Blunkett's contribution, comprising his relationship with the teaching unions, the expansion of the numbers of teachers and teaching assistants, and the Sure Start programme. The eclectic skills, talents and powers that combined to make the office of Secretary for Education and Employment so influential and all-encompassing are revealed in his interview (note that the remit had changed since Lord Baker's period in office), as well as the extended focus on David Blunkett's career and education in Chapter 2 (see 'The Greasy Pole').

3

Limitations on Power

The politicians I interviewed and surveyed expressed what they perceived as limitations on ministers' powers. They also spoke about the barriers ministers face in pursing the policies they wish to adopt. Such restraints are applicable, as we shall see later, to the office environment. A full and clear explanation of such aspects of the political and administrative systems should assist readers in their understanding of the origins of power and authority in corporations and government institutions.

The workings of UK government, and policy-making that take place in the upper echelons of power, are affected, it can be said, by a number of influences, from the priorities and ideas espoused by the prime minister, the cabinet and in the corridors of Whitehall, through the internal workings of political parties and trade unions, to the 'grass roots' represented in meetings or local pressure group activities. Lessons drawn from these sources instruct us how we can conduct ourselves in administrative careers in both the private and public sectors.

The interaction of a number of forces imposes limitations on the power of senior political officers to govern. No matter how domineering a manager can be, we have ways to curb their powers. Where bosses give indiscriminate orders without gaining consensus and without the support and respect of those around them, they are swimming in dangerous waters.

Political Power and Office Politics

When Margaret Thatcher was prime minister, she appointed and supported Kenneth Baker and later Tony Blair appointed and supported David Blunkett. The two education ministers' periods in power were characterised by conflict and controversy, but both ministers were responsible for a number of reforms, and these, and the personalities involved, combine to continue to show us how the operations of government can give us the means to protect ourselves against unscrupulous management.

Where democratic rule is exercised, power apparently resides among the voters, and public opinion has a say in determining outcomes in the political process. In office parlance parallels could be drawn between the electorate and the workforce. But to what extent is the voter or office worker protected? What power do we really have? Casting a vote once every five years and working hard in the office with very little say in how we are governed give very little opportunity to participate in a democracy (if an office is a democracy, about which your views may differ). Democratic participants in Britain are in a position to contribute alongside the functioning of a liberal democracy, a concept that can be observed in the office environment in the sense that we should have rights to equality and fairness in the workplace. But unless we are prepared to play the game and engage in office politics, there might be little hope for the democrat.

Dictatorial rule by business leaders threatens to strike at the very heart of their subordinates' pursuit of happiness. Acceptance of this premise has led to continual debates on the merits and demerits of the way in which behaviour in the office is conducted. As in former times pockets of intense scrutiny exist, but it could be argued that nowadays scrutineers might sometimes have power to act on what they observe. MBA students, when they do their courses, discuss whether managing in a tyrannical fashion does any favours to managers or their staff. Some wrestle with the concept of Karma but repeated examples show that what goes around, comes around. The importance of humanitarian values, underpinned by democratic processes, serve to highlight that our liberal democracy is one to be cherished. Where there is evidence of undesirably severe office politics in organisations, then individuals need to protect their interests lest they become the scapegoat and hence lose their way and ultimately their job.

The relationship between the prime minister and cabinet ministers resembles that between senior and junior managers. David Blunkett is keen to assert that, between the 1997 general election and his first actions in office, much work was done between himself and Tony Blair and the special relationship between them ensured that there was a common purpose. Consider a new director reviewing the line managers in their department, or a new manager reviewing their staff. Where managers cooperate with their subordinates and bring about change in an atmosphere of support and harmony, it is hoped that much can be achieved and the chosen path can add to the satisfaction of all parties. There were on occasions some disagreement between Baker and Blunkett and their respective prime ministers, but overall both ministers initially had a clear direction on policy. Both the 1984 Conservatives and New Labour were voted in with significant majorities so the parties had a strong mandate to govern. When an office worker is newly appointed, they are fresh to the job and they have been voted in by their manager (usually!) and endorsed by HR. I saw how, once newly appointed, Cabinet ministers can draw more effectively on support 'to win over their Department'. However, the Civil Service machine can always put up counter-objectives and represents a curb on ministerial power. Civil servants can go against the wishes of the rulers in the form of bureaucratic obstruction.

Here, then, attention can be given to the expertise of civil servants, who are directly concerned with the day-to-day responsibilities of their department. Office politicians can learn from civil servants who are, it seems, experts in mastering the do's and don'ts of administrative life and in getting their way in the workplace. Office workers are advised to watch the still relevant TV series *Yes Minister/Yes Prime Minister* (available on DVD) to pick up on the daily nuances of power and to observe how they could manipulate their boss if they want to allow their own agenda to come into play.

Written and Unwritten Laws

The position of the Treasury in the power structures within government is of interest for our perceptions of the office environment, if we consider the role of the finance department in companies or public sector entities. They have power over the purse strings and their influence over policy can be disproportionate.

It is as well to focus on processes and institutions in so far as they affect the Prime Minister and the Cabinet, or a manager and a group of employees, and on how conflicts arise and policies are devised. At another level, we can see how values can be teased out and realised in the executive branch of government and draw parallels concerning office work. This objective was best summed up by Maurice Kogan: 'I assume that it is the task of social scientists to take things apart'. Such an approach can inform us better about how to 'adapt and behave as we do our daily tasks in the organisation where we are employed'.[7]

The British constitution, that is the rules of government, serves to protect the individual and society against the excesses of a leadership that threatens to challenge important freedoms held by its citizens. An 'office constitution' can likewise provide protection and act to prevent minorities or victims from being discriminated against or persecuted by corrupt or overbearing management. Both the British constitution and the 'laws' relating to office psychology come in both written and unwritten forms.

---

7   M. Kogan, *The Politics of Education*, London: Penguin, 1971.

In the Office

In government rules and procedures are the essence of the historical nature of the British political system which is inherently
supported by a dependence on a set of fragmented rules and
precedents giving government in the UK the collective right to
serve the people. The absence of any one document that can be
referred to as the constitution led Alexis de Tocqueville to
comment that 'in England, the constitution may change continually, or rather it does not in reality exist'.[8] In commerce, it is
important to establish laws for management to observe. Yet it is
also understood that staff should not step out of line (or, anyway,
not too far or too often).

Staff can restrain management by means of a constitution or set
of rules, whether they are written or unwritten. In an office a
constitution is very largely unwritten: we are subjected to the rules
and principles of an unwritten law. We accept that it is wrong to
bully or to act in a way that ignores certain norms or values. If
staff are gripped by the narcissistic and bully-boy tactics of an
uncompromising boss their lives can be blighted. Where a
manager is bullying you, it is important to set boundaries. One
employee was exploited by her boss who, for example, regularly
demanded she carry out office duties outside her contracted
hours. After declining to do such out-of-hours tasks, she
explained to her superior that he was being unreasonable and as
a result she felt a lot less resentful.[9]

As office staff we can adopt attitudes and behaviour to enhance
our position at work. Michael Foley writes that the constitution
gives emphasis to a government being permitted to govern.[10] In

---

8   A. de Tocqueville, *Democracy in America*, Paris, 1835.

9   K. Dillon, *HBR Guide to Office Politics*, Boston, MA: Harvard Business
Review Press, 2015, pp. 59–60. Such an approach will work in some circumstances and be completely inappropriate in others; the point is how this
employee felt after *succeeding* in setting boundaries.

10   M. Foley, *The Politics of the British Constitution*, Manchester and New
York: Manchester University Press, 1999, p. 2.

the same way, the office rules, breach of which are sometimes codified in employment law and the job contract between employee and employer, consist largely of a body of unwritten laws which determine the way in which administrative life proceeds.[11]

The British constitution has evolved over the years as indeed have office rules. One secretary whose head of department told her that artificial intelligence and word recognition could replace her, demanded whether he wanted 'a smack in the gob'. Maybe you could say that the short exchange was just the usual, light-hearted office banter, but many a true word is said in jest, the head of department was clearly upset and the secretary had breached an unwritten rule. Soon after she was given marching orders in the form of a redundancy notice, even though she was only a year away from retirement. Onlookers believed that the secretary's actions were intended to further her own agenda: subconsciously or consciously, to bring about a fat redundancy cheque. Such are the unwritten rules of office life. The secretary's breach of a boundary could be seen as, in her case, a means to further her own ends and those who wish to get their way might learn a lesson from this (perhaps) ploy.

The importance of a manager stretching out to staff at the bottom of the hierarchy is essential here. Those whose job is essentially to serve others above them must be respected in the same way as the office manager and those others. Everyone below the level of management must consciously be appealed to so that they are motivated and carry with them a definite sense of responsibility within the organisation. The prospect of promotion must loom large and they must be invited to do training, so long as this is within their comfort zone or personal capabilities and does not overstretch them, as this can be counterproductive. On the other side of the coin, the employee

---

11   Of course, many organisations issue a staff handbook; but I will leave it to the reader to decide how completely the staff handbook covers the rules in your own office.

should seek actively to gain better pay and conditions. A journalist-who works in an office environment never fails, at the end of each year, to request a pay rise from his employer. He never takes his foot off the gas, so to speak, and always commits 100% to the assignments he is given. He puts forward his case and is rewarded accordingly with a rise, albeit usually a relatively small one.

But an office worker must realise that if their salary rises too far, there is the danger of pricing oneself above what the market will bear. What if our admin assistant had continually got salary increases over four years and then found that what he was receiving was well over the market rate? He might be 'let go', or even told that his job would be offered at a much lower rate of pay and asked to reapply.

Another 'core' domain concerns the requirement to hold staff appraisals within specified periods, allowing praise or criticism to be given and in a political sense to allow voting on how management and its objectives affect morale and performance.

Personalities

Blunkett has made it clear how much importance he attached to the personality of the minister. His reply here, taken to a micro-level, indicates that managers need to be strong and must ensure that the team around them are capable and able to contribute to the organisation's aims and objectives. There is invariably going to be someone who can be described as the fly in the ointment. In Blunkett's case, Gordon Brown presented 'hiccups' made worse by Brown's special relationship with the prime minister. In any social or business hierarchy there is always a figure going to work against you in whatever you do. It even occurs in families – there is almost always an undesirable who puts a spanner in the works. You just have to proceed in the best way you can. A ruthless dictator, such as Saddam Hussein, would simply murder anyone he saw as a threat to his leadership. In a less brutal way, you can be a victim of your family or their scapegoat, and the same invariably happens in offices so the saying 'you can choose your friends but not your family' can often be extended to 'you can choose your friends but not your work colleagues or manager'. As a manager try to let the individuality of your team members flourish so that yours can also. Blunkett explained: ' . . . the individuals . . . get something out of it, the team undoubtedly get something out of it and therefore the government in terms of implementing policy gets something out it. I think that's a lesson that is often forgotten.'

Another important area of office politics is the organisation's relationship with external parties. Working friendships with people in outside companies can be very rewarding for both sides and lead to mutual satisfaction. They can promote a feeling of trust and bonhomie. Wherever cooperation and harmony are secured between internal and external entities, many beneficial policies can emerge, and office staff can proceed in the knowledge that they have successfully worked with outside parties and be seen to do their work efficiently and effectively.

However, where a clique is established, or an individual is intent on upsetting you, it is helpful to take the politician's approach and to verbally attack the opponent. For example, when I asked Blunkett about Michael Gove, who was the educational secretary at the time of the interview, he called Gove a 'zealot' and somebody who was extremely difficult to 'read' and understand. Blunkett went on to underline Gove's 'ideological obsession'. Where you wish to form your own private circle, then do not hesitate to meet over coffee or somewhere in private to bitch about those who are annoying you. In the office, getting back at a person who has upset you is arguably best achieved by gossip. And if you can effectively take the mickey out of your enemy then this could be helpful too. The outcome might be seen as basic office banter, but as I quoted above, 'many a true word is spoken in jest'. For those with a strong sense of morality or religious beliefs such underhand tactics may be out of the question but if the alternative is to be the office scapegoat such action can in many ways be justified. In the office, it is survival of the fittest, so if you have deep humanitarian principles, then move on and search for another job or career. It's a hard fact of life though that running away is really not the best policy, since you may move to a different kind of job and find that you are still being shot at or undermined.

A final note about dealing with exploitation in the office. If you find yourself in this position and you stand up for yourself, as with the bargaining and negotiation which are a part of the life of the whips in Parliament, hold out for the best deal and maximise any benefits that might come your way. It is interesting to note that MPs are now less deferential than they used to be. Why not take a leaf out of their book and try not to be squashed by management, without going so far as to appear rude or arrogant; instead, show that you can be assertive.

Above all, do not let managers bully or take advantage of you. Where there is a clause in your contract that says that you are expected to carry out other duties considered reasonable in the context of the job, never fail to mention the importance of the term 'reasonable'. Where coerced into extra work, set boundaries and do not let these be broken.

The Greasy Pole: Lessons from David Blunkett's Career

Where office employees are determined to rise to the top, they can learn from politics. They must seek to become a 'national figure' and so adopt delusions of grandeur. In that role, the employee's mental picture is distorted: (s)he sees his or her contribution as indispensable to the office, and the office as crucial to their goal in life.

In his rise to the top, David Blunkett adopted an authoritative style and, by the early 1980s, his position as leader of Sheffield Council had begun to propel him to national fame. In the office you should commit totally to your work and endeavour to be friendly with your colleagues, but not try to always gain favour with management, or risk being accused of sucking up. Where you are more introverted, such a course may not suit your personality. In such a case, you must accept that you might never be promoted, and your purpose is to work behind the scenes. However, it is best not to rule yourself out totally; later, an opportunity to change tack may come. Outside events, e.g. a bereavement, might force you to change course and this may dent your confidence and temporarily cause you to avoid the fray. If you are ever invited to give a presentation, it is important to be thoroughly prepared. The prospect of having to appear on TV filled Blunkett with horror. His audience enjoyed his performance and he was able to ensure that he was invited back on the programme on subsequent occasions.[12] Fame was not far away, and he was climbing the political ladder rung by rung.

To maintain momentum is important. Try to be understanding of your colleagues, offering sympathy in facing their woes and troubles and praise for whatever they are doing or hope to do, without either flattering them or taking sides. Where you are unable to gain the support of all, which is normally the case, seek to form a clique by which you are part of the group in ascendency. Push to one side unwanted comments and circulate within your chosen circle. In an office hierarchy, a clerk did her best to 'send to Coventry' one unpopular character within her office; she would talk only to her own supporters; but by doing this she gave the scapegoat enough rope to hang her (she was 'let go').

Blunkett also realised the importance of doing well in committees and meetings. His membership of the Labour Party's National Executive Committee (NEC) is a case in point. Offering a unique platform, the NEC allowed Blunkett to become a nationally recognised figure. Where there are office meetings, attempt, if you can, to assert yourself and contribute in a meaningful way to the discussions. Even if you lack qualifications or experience push yourself forward, if you can, but

---

12   D. Blunkett and A. McCormick, *On a Clear Day*, London: Michael O'Mara Books, 1995, p. 151.

without stepping too much on the toes of your colleagues. Blunkett was the first non-MP since the 1940s to be elected a member of the NEC.[13] In any speech or presentation, Blunkett did his homework thoroughly. Always prepare well. When you know what is to be discussed, then ensure you are familiar with the topic inside out. Do not hesitate to take the lead in debate and seize your opportunities when they come. In securing promotion, bide your time and when the moment is ripe act quickly. Blunkett was fortunate that his timing was perfect as when he put himself forward for election to the NEC there were (unusually) two vacancies, one of which had been created by Neil Kinnock being elected leader of the Labour Party. As Stephen Pollard recalls, Blunkett did not have to unseat anyone, and this allowed delegates something of a free vote.[14] In your office, try to keep off the subjects of politics or religion. You must not seem be a political optimist or calculator, even though nothing might be further from your personal position. Come from behind and act as a dark horse. Show your interest in what people have to say. And above all ensure that your work is of a high standard. You may, if you are cautious, attempt to give orders to your colleagues and thus show your that you have leadership skills (management potential) but be very careful here. In one office, a junior employee used to boss his co-workers about. Usually such behaviour is intolerable in an organisational setting, but surprisingly it worked here, and the underling secured a promotion and was given supervisory responsibilities. But within less than a year he had to find new employment, whether for higher pay, better prospects or simply because his inability to cope had come to light is uncertain.

What other lessons can we learn from David Blunkett? Colleagues always found him very frank and he answered media questions to the best of his ability. In view of his visual impairment, he made considerable advances over the years, and you could not help but think that if he had not been blind he might

---

13   Harold Laski, professor of politics at the London School of Economics. See S. Pollard, *David Blunkett*, p. 114.
14   Ibid., p. 115.

have made it to the premiership. On the other hand, maybe this was part and parcel of his success. A blind lady who was an administrator and gave excellent presentations during her work never got nervous beforehand and once said she could not see anyone in the audience, so it was like giving a talk in a quiet room with nobody present. She was highly intelligent, and she coped very well despite her disability.

The inability to see had completely taken over in David's life. From the age of 4 he attended a residential home for blind children. This cut him off from his family and peer group but, in his words, it made him very 'robust'. He had to fend for himself and, being away from home, it taught him at a very early age to do practical tasks: cleaning his shoes, making his own bed and generally looking after himself. That self-reliance and resilience were clearly a grounding and a foundation for later life, which for office staff goes to show how resourceful we can be when the going gets rough. In times of adversity, with everyday pressures made worse through illness, we can learn from David what can be done. With the support of a personal assistant, Mandy Maddocks (the blind advocate I mentioned in Chapter 1) was able to perform what would have been an extremely complex job for anyone and the pair of them, for example, tackled the administrative work in her department very efficiently. This is a lesson for those with visual impairment and shows there is still the option to pursue a constructive career, and take advantage of schemes intended to provide help (for example, Blunkett found that in south London funding for employing a PA was available).

To those who seek top administrative work, David is an inspiration. At the age of 16 he had no formal qualifications. Office staff who can only obtain low-grade work can take a leaf out of David's book. He went to evening classes and, once he had got a job in his home city of Sheffield, he persuaded his employer to agree to his going one day a week to college. It should be noted, however, that day release can be a two-edged sword: in one respect it is a cost-effective way to gain qualifications that can assist in achieving promotion and enabling you to do your job better, particularly if you do vocational courses in office admin. Yet the time to go to college could rile your colleagues back in the office, especially if you are the only one having 'a day off' and you are learning something which would help you stand out against them in the promotion stakes.

David got his employer to fund a day a week at college and he arranged to do two additional classes a week. Such a heavy programme of learning can be tiring. This kind of workload/study is reminiscent of the private teachers in Victorian England: but many of them barely had the energy to attend evening classes and the cost of studying in the evenings was often beyond their reach. David's heavy study schedule enabled him to pass some O Levels, then some A Levels and a National Certificate in Business Studies. Office workers who seek to qualify in this way might follow a similar path.

To digress, let us look at the example of an administrative career in the civil service, where qualifications could very much help in gaining promotion or applying for jobs. Administrative officers will need at least 5 GCSEs, including maths and English, and many candidates applying for the same jobs may have two or more A Levels or a degree. So someone, like David Blunkett, with few or no qualifications might appear to be at quite a disadvantage. However, some departments do not require specific qualifications and instead allow applicants to sit aptitude tests in areas such as teamwork, communication skills, knowledge and behaviour, that test whether you hold values set by the civil service.[15] Open competition based on individual merit is a principle dating from the nineteenth century, and has been a benchmark that the Civil Service has very much wanted to preserve and protect. On some occasions, such as for temporary appointments, the Civil Service Commission has been lenient and has allowed exceptions to its own requirements.[16] This

---

15 *Careers 2016*, 12th edition, Surbiton: Trotman Education, 2015, p. 13.
16 R. Willis, *Testing Times: A history of vocational, civil service, and secondary examinations in England since 1850*, Rotterdam: Sense Publishers, 2013, p. 143.

concession is to be noted, since the aptitude tests are objectively quite hard to pass and even graduates have often failed at this stage. It might well be that temporary employment in the Civil Service can also lead to a permanent appointment.

After David's National Certificate, it took him six years to acquire the qualifications to enrol at the University of Sheffield. Office staff may well think it best to by-pass university but after a handful of exam passes they could well consider going for an HND/HNC in business management, which equates in level to a pass degree and which now in fact represents two years of a three-year degree in business studies. Such an award can be gained through day release or evening study (or both, bearing in mind David's example).

In the office, much can be done by the candidate to pave the way for promotion. Where they are diligent, they are in full view of management and once a vacancy comes up, they stand a good chance of success. One office clerk worked conscientiously for one year, saying very little to her colleagues during the day. She made a good impression in the eyes of her manager and was promoted from clerical officer to higher clerical officer (HCO) despite having few paper qualifications. In the same organisation another HCO clearly had potential to be promoted, but always failed because once, in a fit of rage, he had poured a pint of beer over the head of one of the directors! The lesson here is never to express anger to anyone you work for, and particularly not your boss; though this might seem something that goes without saying, it often seems to be a trap that the reckless fall into.

Before the 1997 General Election David spent much time with Tony Blair, so much so that promotion to the full Cabinet when New Labour came into power was inevitable. A lot of preparation had been done before that general election; David considered himself to be very fortunate in the sense that Blair had evaluated his talent before appointing him to the post of Shadow Education Secretary and subsequently Education and Employment Secretary once in government. Proving that it is important for the office employee not to always be a 'yes man', David admitted that he did not always share a common purpose with Tony Blair and that they did not always agree. What the two politicians did share was a common direction and as a result the prime minister gave David a wide brief, which worked to the education secretary's advantage.

As far as promotion is concerned, if you do take on more responsibility you must be able to cope with the increased duties and be able to (or learn to) delegate. Generally, at an interview the interviewers will seek to assess the suitability of the candidate for promotion and, if they have already been scrutinised in the work they have been doing managers should know whether the interviewee meets the specified criteria. This, however, may not always be the case. As Blunkett's number two, Estelle Morris was very effective in taking action where local authorities were clearly failing to give the necessary drive and support for the changes that were required. She became a minister in the Department for Education and Employment in 1997 and was promoted to Secretary of State for Education and Skills in 2001. Out of the blue, she suddenly resigned her post in October 2002, explaining that she did not feel up to the job. In interviews after her resignation she disclosed that she had felt more contented and more effective as a junior education minister. This is an example of someone slipping through the net, yet it is an obvious case of a promotion going wrong. A hospital sister was promoted to the admin post of nursing officer – away from the wards and from patient care, she soon resigned from her position, acknowledging that her new office role did not suit her.

4

Exercises of Power

The problem of 'elective dictatorship', which has a bearing on offices in that managers may abuse the power they have, was a distinctive feature of Thatcher's and Blair's governments, signalling that once elected or appointed ministers were given too much freedom to do what they wanted irrespective of their staff or the voting public. Despite pervasive criticism at almost every level, the PM or manager is presented with the powers to bring in change. Those who favour a diminution of power may do so for self-interested motives – still, control rests with management and where it is forceful much can be achieved. Nonetheless, it must be remembered that staff and voters can always vote with their feet.

In the UK managers are not elected to office. On a kibbutz in Israel a Marxist system is used and managers work on a temporary basis, later giving way to others. Office staff in Britain and Europe are rarely given the power to elect their managers and have to face whoever is in post. That is not to say that all (or even many) managers are undesirables; only that, where an undesirable holds authority subordinates must repel that unsavoury leader by ganging up with other staff to make a case for dismissing or demoting the manager in post. When Margaret Thatcher was in Paris her leadership was put in jeopardy when some of her colleagues conspired to get rid of her. A sustained attack resulted in her having to resign, and so pave the way for John Major to take the helm. Likewise, a nurse who, after years serving as a staff nurse, was appointed to sister-grade, proved to be such a tartar that her nursing subordinates combined to appeal to the directors to sack her: she was demoted. Here as well as in the office unity of this kind can be maintained and the wishes of the staff can be instrumental in a higher-ranking authority (or a prime minister) being removed.

Political scientists observe an oppressor/oppressed cycle, in which once an oppressor is overcome the oppressed take up the mantle and continue to exploit their peers. The new leadership proves to be as perverse as the toppled oppressor. In the office, when a power struggle arises, eventually a new regime may occupy the seat of power: but how often are their colours really different?

Quiet Revolutions

When the doctrine that 'we'd better all be in the same story' is applied to the office, how responsible is the manager in post? How free is (s)he to exploit staff? Should (s)he be allowed to constantly frustrate and annoy them? One example was when an administrator ordered stationery – he would show his boss the list of required pens, batteries, paper clips, etc., but his manager would always disagree with the list of items to be ordered that week. This stance undermined the administrator's sense of well-being. The way out of this situation was for him to stop showing the list to his manager. This worked: the manager never interfered again.

In a UK company, an obnoxious secretary made the life of other secretaries and admin staff in the office a misery. She thought she was a cut above everyone else, as she had a degree; she was a complete narcissist. On one occasion she even used physical force to repel someone she did not like. Her colleagues conspired to get rid of her, by either ignoring or actively upsetting her as she went about her daily tasks. Following a barrage of criticism and abuse, she resigned, or was effectively 'sacked' from her job. In the aftermath of this episode the outgoing secretary wrote to the office manager, criticising the main contributors to her downfall. The head seemingly sought no disciplinary actions against the accused and perhaps he was as thankful for her departure as the rest of the office staff had been. However, the band of office staff responsible for the secretary's departure later lost their own jobs, which maybe points to a worldly justice having the last say.

Harmful behaviour can have recurring repercussions. Excessive micky-taking can have dire consequences yet, where the victim can laugh off any unwanted provocation, they can win through and save the day. One manager in a finance department set out to torment one of his staff by sellotaping one of his costings to the celling. The victim simply laughed off the 'joke' and in doing so found that the abuse came to an end. Subsequently he was accepted as part of the team; had he given signs that he was upset perhaps the bullying would have continued. There was no guarantee that treating this unacceptable behaviour as a joke would cause it to stop. It may have been the case that explicit criteria for legal action would not have been met; or, in other words, that no written law could have been called in aid to put an end to the torment, so such a solution would have been difficult to find. But it must be remembered that the British constitution does contain *some* written laws to defend its subjects; but this was clearly not an option that the victim chose to take up. Indeed, the absence of a single, unified set of laws bearing on office behaviour has not led to ungovernable actions at work.

Another approach is to seek help from your manager, who may be able to come up with a workable solution. A financial administrator was bullied after one of her colleagues failed to get a temporary posting to Australia. After being physically mauled and verbally abused, the victim complained to her manager, and the bully was transferred out of the office to a different site. You do not have to resort to underhand behaviour in situations like this, and you are free to choose how to react.

Failures of Communication and Unintended Consequences

Much scorn was heaped on a young man working as a temp in London by the permanent staff, who took a dislike of the newcomer; it may have been because they knew he was well qualified but, for whatever reason, he was unpopular. The organisation hired him for many weeks and clearly the management were happy with the work he was doing. He was glad when a full-time, permanent vacancy in a similar line of work became available. As a trusted worker, seen as doing a good job, he applied for the post and was duly interviewed. He did not get the post. Mistakenly and through no fault of his own, he later found out, the interviewers had thought he was a qualified chartered secretary – a high-ranking diploma in commerce, both in the private and public sectors – and so, overqualified. Perhaps if he had been more liked by more of the other staff, he might have secured the post. But if you are one of those who often fail at interviews, the setback can be a blessing in disguise; in this case, the temp went on to find better and higher-paid work elsewhere.

A manager was in strong alliance with the company secretary and PA to the boss. This manager was on a personal mission to make almost the entire administrative staff leave. He wanted above anything else to have a young female secretary and would reduce his older secretary to tears on a regular basis. One of the clerks took a stand and argued to him that he should be less aggressive towards his secretary; the outcome was that that clerk was made redundant!

5

Change and Reform

Reform and change can be as much a feature of government as it is in office life. An elected House of Lords, fewer MPs and equal-sized constituencies, fixed-term Parliaments, powers to recall MPs, elected Select Committee chairmen are just some of the constitutional issues on the political agenda. The barrage of recommendations for constitutional reappraisal is vast. In the office world, much can be said about the introduction of changes. Sometimes the leadership effects change in order to retain control. They do not want their staff to become complacent, while desiring efficiency to be achieved at almost any cost.

In politics a lesson here is that when reform is extensive, a radical party runs the risk of unpopularity. Many asserted that the Coalition Government's programme lacked a coherent strategic approach. The penalty was paid by the Liberal Democrats, who made a very poor showing at the general election in 2015. Despite the Leave vote in the Brexit referendum, subsequently Brexit lost popular favour, and UKIP have paid the price.

Where managers spend time developing new systems but these do not take on then it is good to wind down the reform. A new relational database system was introduced by an oil company, but because staff did not learn or use it to the full, the leadership team eventually decided to put an end to it, despite much financial investment to get the scheme up and working. New Labour put much energy into forming a General Teaching Council but, as Blunkett said, it disappointed its sponsors, who had hoped it would play a much bigger part in teachers' professional development and the standing of the teaching profession.[17]

Change and Reform

Positive promises can often lose momentum after the planning stage when leaderships attempt to introduce them. Certain reversals of New Labour's constitutional laws are a case in point: the proposal to introduce ID cards, for example, was scrapped amid a cry for a restoration of liberties. In national politics there can be an engagement in horse-trading in which principles of fairness and social justice are falsely bandied about in favour of bringing about desirable change.

In writing this I aim to give a background to some of the concepts that can drive political democracy to apply to offices in the modern era. It was within these constraints that Kenneth Baker and David Blunkett operated and launched educational reform and they did this in a system run by an unwritten constitution, in which the notion of 'elective dictatorship' prevailed. It was their intention to bring about radical changes that struck at the heart of school, college and university administration. They resolved to alter the framework of our educational system and to introduce shifts in power through important Parliamentary legislation. Where there is no shortage of enthusiasm and confidence, a powerful management team can act to win over the hearts and minds of their staff, who enter into a kind of contract, allowing them to absorb some change but at the same time make way for other changes to the way in which the organisation performs. Where managers succeed in carrying out such an process, society can prosper and conflict can be kept to a minimum in order to bring about success and improve profitability. While talks are in progress, the door is opened to challenges and the true value of sustaining a regulatory

---

17   R. Willis, *The Struggle for the General Teaching Council*, London and New York: Routledge/Falmer, 2005.

imbalance of powers is opened to question: some will assert an executive claim to govern while not necessarily upholding the status quo, others will seek to curb such claims.

Brexit has fostered divisions and acrimony among politicians and the public, both within and outside the UK. The furore was weaker during Baker's and Blunkett's periods in government yet through force of personality they brought about changes that had been set out in their parties' manifestos. In education Blunkett was able to say that there was absolutely no opposing influence elsewhere. Since action was mutual, he felt free to try to drive more radical changes, such as to the Lisbon Treaty in 2000 and his efforts to attempt to free up the labour market. Blunkett is defensive in this part of my interview with him, but he was right to assert that the European Union itself and the European Commission had very little influence over the Labour Government's policies in education. While opponents have claimed that the EU intrudes into many key areas of domestic policy, setting the National Curriculum and dictating the way in which the teaching profession evolved (to take two examples) were policies that remain outside the Union's sphere of activity.

Any regulatory reforms can be legitimised by referendum, which is evident in the case of Brexit, and thus can often be observed in the form of or stakeholder interventions in the business of companies, partnerships and public sector organisations. It is worth here referring to the work of Karl Marx. I argue that company bosses can achieve nothing without their workers and vice versa: likewise, Marx rightly showed that capitalists cannot live without the proletariat. Constitutional reform may arrive at the behest of shareholders (which are often companies whose policy is made by their directors), or trade unions (which represent their members), or other people or bodies that have a stake in an organisation (such as its staff) or a government (such as an electorate).

Takeovers and Mergers

Administrative change in the office when a company merger takes place, for example, often sees political opposition at its worst and callously presents management determined to cling to power, irrespective of the wishes of their staff, who may even lose their jobs because redundancy is planned.

Despite any important new changes to the way in which the organisation operates, change should not be regarded as totally undesirable. One argument goes that groups or cliques in an office might have sponsored an oppressive environment that usurped the principles of fairness and social justice within the corporation: so not all would not be lost where radical reform followed a takeover or merger. And where the manager or staff does lose their job, the Invisible Hand of the market can find them in more amenable and sometimes even better-paid employment.

Everyday Change and Reform

Where management that has the general support of its employees imposes reform from above, this does not necessarily entail losing that support, but perhaps it might need to seek alliances with more subordinate individuals or groupings working in the organisation. However, where favour is seen to extend to them, then such individuals or groups may become unpopular with colleagues, as preferential treatment by the leadership can be seen as unfair. The manager of a department wanted to build an effective team, but sadly he applied the 'divide and rule' approach. He did his best to split up the team since, in his view, if they conflicted with one another they would turn to work with more rigour and efficiency.

By contrast, David Blunkett recognised the importance of building a supportive team around him, united in common purpose. The unity he achieved among his team ensured that he and they had a clearer perspective and understanding; this was especially true in the field of early years' education. The benefits of a unified and determined approach were evident when the Labour government under Tony Blair introduced its first education White Paper, which was developed and put before the House of Commons within 63 days – this was a record. Moreover the speed with which the White Paper was put into action was remarkable.

Michael Moran, a political analyst, suggests that rules can be dreamt up by whichever group is the most powerful.[18] The way employees react is not fiction. The work of Walter Bagehot is cited in support of Moran's thesis.[19] The constitution is invoked as a symbol commanding loyalty and as a practical means of specifying the game of government.[20] Likewise, a manager can manage by utilising similar components of obedience.

It is true that managers' actions can be interpreted as having a desired meaning for a given group, but interpretation is not necessarily the same as control over the way a leadership governs. Still, intervention is always possible and in some areas may pose more threat to the leadership than in others. It is thus important to distinguish between core domains of the reform and contested domains, often in the unwritten rules governing how a manager should act. Governments cannot expressly act in direct contravention of the law and they operate in accordance with the courts and legislative activity within Parliament. Managers must listen to the concerns of their staff and riding roughshod over the wishes of the majority can have unexpected consequences. Constraints on policy have existed not just through institutions such as the European Union, but also in the work of citizens and pressure

---

18   M. Moran, *Politics and Governance in the UK*, Basingstoke: Palgrave Macmillan, 2005, p. 77.
19   W. Bagehot, *The English Constitution*, London: Chapman & Hall, 1867. Republished with an index and a student guide to further reading, introduced by Gavin Phillipson. Brighton: Sussex Academic Press, 1997.
20   M. Moran, *Politics and Governance in the UK*, Basingstoke: Palgrave Macmillan, 2005, p. 77.

groups who are active in the courts.[21] While the typical office setup does not allow interest and pressure groups to dominate, the leadership nevertheless would be unwise not to bow to the interests of their staff.

A training company tried to introduce some new courses. The training manager liaised with the head of department in trying to formulate a new set of diplomas. The manager first outlined his intentions and then provided more detail in a discussion document. He allowed for alternatives so that the committee charged with the ultimate decision did not feel that their options were narrow ones. He met a committee member and succeeded in winning him over; then consulted other members of the committee in the same way. Note how this behind-the-scenes politicking helped to muster support, in a way very like how the Whips' Office wins Parliamentary votes before MPs go through the division lobbies in the House of Commons. The committee accepted that the training manager's recommendations for the diplomas seemed to be the best way forward and his lobbying and research helped him to present evidence to support his goals. Eventually, the committee accepted the proposal.

New Blood and Old Hands

It is interesting that an office worker when starting a job can work very enthusiastically and productively once the initial problems of settling into the workplace are overcome. The best work is normally done in the first year: a peak of performance is achieved within that period. From that point onwards, there is the possibility of a downward spiral and of the employee losing interest in the job. They can be bogged down with excessive work, subject to the vagaries of office politics. Mary Wildman, a former teacher, when interviewed explained that it is better in the admin field only to stay in the same job for two years. She

---

21   Ibid.

admitted that initially a new job creates new problems at first but that these are only temporary and once they are overcome the newcomer can gain far more job satisfaction and enjoyment than incumbents do. Both the Thatcher and Blair administrations, having been in office for too long, became stale and in need of a period in opposition to recharge their batteries.

Where you work in a team, it is essential that everyone is pulling their weight and working towards commonly held objectives. David Blunkett very much benefited from the cooperation of the Permanent Secretary, Sir Michael Bichard, who displayed great enthusiasm. A manager wants a team that can perform and deliver the goods, so to speak. David had an extremely well versed and experienced team round him who were committed to the agenda of raising standards and of improvement, which fitted in well with Blair's mantra 'Education, Education, Education'.

After making sure they have an adept team around them, management must fill the team's days by enthusing, motivating and setting a good example in their leadership role. Mandy Maddocks (the blind advocate I mentioned in Chapters 1 and 3), when working in local government, was a very astute advisor to the head of department, who particularly valued her contribution and the advice she gave enabled him to promote his leadership role within the organisation. David Blunkett elaborated on the importance of having the right team around him. He could rely on the 'credibility' of the government advisor, Professor Michael Baber.[22] Michael understood the importance of his role and how best to ensure that policy was both appreciated and well informed. So Blair and Blunkett worked together in partnership; they enjoyed a honeymoon phase, with the press off their backs. They had a fresh mandate from the nation and they were full of enthusiasm; but eventually, the team became worn out and subject to bitter attacks from the press. Blair is now remembered, more than anything else, for his mistake in

---

22 Whose colleagues, including Professor Brian Holmes, I used to work with at the Institute of Education, University College London.

waging war with Saddam Hussein; like all prime ministers, he lost his popularity.

Where the head of department feels that (s)he is losing the plot, and that there are motivational problems with staff, arranging a special away day where staff and management can try to address some of the management problems that are holding back progress may be a way forward. Such an exercise can allow the head to display prowess – strong communication skills, perhaps – and to attempt to iron out particular problems. Managing can be a daunting task. As already mentioned, at the beginning of a project there normally is great keenness to make a success of what the organisation has set out to do. New Labour decided that, alongside economic recovery and employment issues, putting education at the centre of government policy and thus achieving reform were central to the way in which the Cabinet wanted to proceed. The school heads, teachers in the classroom and teacher unions knew that Blunkett meant business and that he had backing from 10 Downing Street.

My interview with David Blunkett gives an interesting account but one in which a favourable picture was presented. He considered relationships in positive terms and explains how everything went right or according to plan. For instance, he asserted that, unless he had won over the Prime Minister and the Permanent Secretary in the Education Department during the first few days of the new government, his Standards and Effectiveness Unit would have died a death. To maintain control managers must always present a united front and appear to be on top of their remit, confident, powerful, adept at speaking, negotiating and explaining. A senior executive from a major high street retail business, when his staff asked how he was, would always reply with the word 'Wonderful' and really mean it. He had no educational qualifications so his determination to remain strong in relation to his office colleagues was always very apparent. As a narcissist, he would perceive no possibility of challenge and he drilled himself to appear perfect to his subordinates and superiors alike.

In *Office Politics* Oliver James writes about the dangers of narcissists, arguing that '[t]he costs of their impulsivity and short-termism are often borne by others, as well as themselves, so that they are . . . aggressive, prone to commit assaults and to perpetrating white-collar crime'.[23] The problem is that, though it is believed that they amount to around one percent of the population, they tend to be overly represented in offices and can have a disastrous impact on the feelings and morale of their subordinates. It can really be said that they are, sadly, an occupational hazard to those that they encounter.

The interview process does not always select the best candidate. The manager who always replied 'wonderful' would not fill a vacancy within his office with anyone he regarded as overqualified. Perhaps he feared to employ a junior who for whatever reason might threaten his ability to lead. When recruiting a secretary, he wanted a novice without many qualifications but who could do the job adequately. Employing a graduate secretary was not on his agenda.

The ability of David Blunkett to form a common front was paramount. He made sure that, with the support of the Leadership Team in his Department, there was an understanding between his own special advisers and the Educational Ministerial Team. In retrospect, his rhetoric illuminated his position and gave the idea that he was in charge and that almost everything went to plan. He was determined to affect the direction of policy, thrashing out where policy was immediately feasible and where his staff needed to do more work. That was then transmitted, both through the message that his colleagues would put out, and through the knowledge that it would have the backing of all the players involved. David's message was optimistic; office workers and, particularly, managers must realise that they really should not reveal negative feelings or opinions, or give examples of past failures. These might undermine their position, or convey defeat. That clearly we all fail

---

23   O. James, *Office Politics*, London: Vermillion, 2013, p. 48.

sometimes cannot be denied, but keep this to yourself and try not to spill the beans. Present an image where you are seen to be indestructible. However, such an approach should not be allowed to spill over to family life. Some managers, particularly after they retire, can behave at home as they did in the office and then all hell is let loose. Frustrated that they are no longer engaged in one-upmanship at work, they can resort to playing games in the private lives of their family members.

David Blunkett spoke about civil servants' roles as experts. He encouraged his staff to focus on expertise and to pursue it for the purposes of promotion. He suggested that the problem of the Civil Service was that staff feel that their prospects for promotion and elevation lie in moving quickly between jobs, demonstrating a breadth of experience rather than a depth of knowledge about an area of administrative work.

While discussing experts, I will spend a little time thinking about the typical accounts department. The significance of the accounts department and the importance of maintaining a good relationship with them is vital, a theme touched upon earlier. The accountant can be a strange breed. One finance clerk took deep pleasure in finding fault with the work of an administrative officer in another department. This was a cynical exercise of power and the clerk got much satisfaction from it. David Blunkett commented, on a similar topic, that it was very difficult to deal with the Treasury because of the power structures within government; the same applies generally to finance departments in the public and private sectors. Where the staff have the backing of the head of their department important inroads can be made. David was very fortunate, it appears, in that he had the backing of the Prime Minister and the two of them, linked to Gordon Brown in the Exchequer, were able to form a triangle which gave David the necessary political clout for his policies to succeed. As is the case with company budgeting, a harmonious relationship with the accounts or finance department is essential; David commented that because the Treasury held the purse strings, they should never be underestimated. Even he admitted that later his relationship with Gordon Brown became difficult, because the Chancellor appeared to be more concerned about the financial implications of child care than with the practical benefits of Sure Start and other child development policies.

In certain posts, e.g. office manager, it is vital to have a knowledge of accounting, and if you do not possess such knowledge, find out whether there is a course that will bring you up to speed. One office manager had no knowledge of budgeting and this annoyed the head of department so much that compulsory redundancy was imposed on her. No matter how difficult the head of department can be, every move should be made to ensure that your work is up to standard and where there are deficiencies to ensure that these are addressed. Powers of persuasion can play an important part here: for example, the Education Maintenance Allowances that David Blunkett greatly favoured would not have been introduced had he not convinced Gordon Brown that committing to getting young people to stay on in education after the age of 16 was absolutely crucial to developing skills, and therefore growth and a modern, global economy.

If you are considering moving to work in accounts, be aware that to some the work can seem boring (though others can find it quite exciting). The intense examinations structure and the need to concentrate hard within the office and master detail can be daunting. A useful qualification which carries much weight is that provided by the Association of Accounting Technicians. Success in these exams can open doors and they are highly rated. Besides, there are those who are happy with number crunching, are able to see past the numbers to what they represent and derive satisfaction from this kind of office work.

David did not conceal his clashes with Gordon Brown in the Treasury and perhaps this is another lesson: try to avoid conflict with members of the accounts department in the office context. David admitted that Gordon did not like him intervening and getting involved with the Monetary Policy Committee of the Bank of England, even though monetary policy has a major impact on employment and skills, so really was an essential aspect of his brief.

6

Case Study: The John Lewis Partnership

Putting powers back in the hands of staff has been apparent in the case of the office workers and retail staff of the John Lewis Partnership, founded by John Spedan Lewis in 1928. He set up a power base that was commercially viable and at the same time 'democratic', giving each employee a share in the business they co-owned.[24] The end product is truly a partnership, allowing management to be entrepreneurial and staff to share in the ownership and running of the organisation.

The financial gains here are likely to improve the productivity of employees, who become more efficient and satisfied in their job as they perceive that hard work will result in higher financial gain and personal reward. I came across a former employee of John Lewis who lives near to Sloane Square in London. She enjoys a comfortable retirement, having worked for the Partnership in Victoria as a senior administrator – she was always full of praise for John Lewis and expressed great admiration for the 'checks and balances' in the way self-governance operated there.

---

24   Available from www.johnlewispartnership.co.uk/about/ our-founder.html, accessed 02/09/2018.

Appendix

Interviews with Lord (David) Blunkett and Lord (Kenneth) Baker

The Rt Hon. David, Lord Blunkett

Willis: Hello.

Blunkett: Hi Richard.

Willis: Hi David Blunkett. Is it okay if I call you David?

Blunkett: Yes it is.

Willis: Well thank you very much for agreeing to chat with me today David. I feel very honoured. I'm recording this conversation.

Blunkett: Of course.

Willis: The date is Monday 21 October 2013 and the time is 11:45 a.m. Have I mentioned when I wrote to you in July and August of this year, the aim of the work is to model it along the lines of the book *The Politics of Education: Edward Boyle and Anthony Crosland in Conversation with Maurice Kogan* published by Penguin in 1974. The chat in short is intended to analyse the role of the Education Minister and to see how your experiences in Government shed light on this role. Some of the answers to these questions may appear in existing publications. My aim here is to stick to Kogan's format so quite clearly other sources may contain the answers.

Blunkett: Of course and that is absolutely fine as long as they're accurately reflected.

Willis: Excellent. It is my intention to have a complete record for the purposes of the book I intend to write and to include the transcript hopefully of your conversation this morning. So is it okay to kick off David?

Blunkett: Yes please do.

Willis: Thank you. What would you say draws men and women to the often precarious and dicey career of the politician?

Blunkett: Well in my case and I think in most cases, it's a genuine desire to make a difference to change the world for the better. Whilst we might have very different approaches and different opinions on how that could be achieved. In my case, my background, the death of my father when I was 12 years old in a works accident, the poverty my mother experienced, the surroundings I grew up in and the experience I had as a blind child in terms of education which was exclusive rather than inclusive, all of those obviously make a difference to your perspective. Mine was that I simply wanted to see the world a lot better than the one I'd experienced as a child.

Willis: Could you say a little more please about your choice of career as determined by family and social background?

Blunkett: Well I was from the age of four at a residential boarding school for blind children. Whilst that had major disadvantages in cutting you off from your family and peer group, it also made you very robust. You had to fend for yourself, you had to learn to do the practical things at a very early age of cleaning your shoes, making your own bed, looking after your-self. That self-reliance and resilience obviously was a grounding and a foundation for later life. But it did in terms of my desire to change the world initially make me want to get involved in education.

After a very difficult start, because at the age of 16 I had no formal qualifications at all because the school I went to had a head teacher who himself had a PhD but didn't think that blind children could usefully undertake formal examinations. I went to evening class and once I'd got a job back in my home city of Sheffield, I got my employer to agree to me going a day a week to college. My quid pro quo was two nights a week at college. Between the day a week and the two nights a week I built up firstly what were then O Levels and then A Levels combined with a National Certificate in Business Studies.

So it took me six years to get the qualifications to get in the University of Sheffield. I wanted to be a teacher and when I got my degree I did a Postgraduate Teaching Certificate for teaching in post-16 educa-tion. I did that simultaneously with having been elected to Sheffield City Council while I was still a student at university.

Willis: Now turning to the post of Education Secretary itself, how did you spend your day as Education Secretary and what was a typical day in your life as Education Minister?

Blunkett: A lot of preparation had been done before the 1997 General Election so I was very fortunate, firstly, in the sense that Tony Blair had tested out with me before giving me the job of Shadow Education and then subsequently Education and Employment Secretary. Whether he and I had common purpose, whether we understood each other, not that we necessarily always agreed but that we had a clear direction, and he therefore gave me a fairly wide brief to be able to get on with the job which is always advantageous.

I saw in opposition the importance of building up an advisory team around me, not just those who I employed eventually as special advisors – excellent as they were – but actually people in the service, people with radical ideas, those who were implementing change. That coterie of expertise was crucial to getting the policies right in opposition and then having a very clear perspective on how to implement them because policies in a vacuum are intellectually stimulating and practically useless.

So it was very important to link what – where we were going and what we wanted to do with hard edge policies. The most obvious examples of these would be early year's education, the development of Sure Start, the first ever National Nursery Education Programme, then the Literacy and Numeracy Strategies which led to the Literacy and Numeracy Hours which we developed in opposition. We came in with the ability to develop the first Education White Paper of the new Government within seven weeks of – well in the end it took us nine weeks, it took us 63 days to get the White Paper in front of the House of Commons which was a record. Then to start the legislative process on the back of changes that didn't need legislation.

So the first period of time was obviously spent ensuring that the Civil Service knew what our programme was, developing a new Standards and Effectiveness Unit which was headed by Professor Sir Michael Barber. The intention there was to get people into the Department for Education and Employment and who had some hands on experience in school, as school leaders, in Local

Government, in academia, who were hands on and therefore bringing something to the table more than just historic policy developers or pen pushers.

We were able to do that with the cooperation of the Permanent Secretary now Lord Michael Bichard – Sir Michael Bichard at the time – who was very enthusiastic. David Normington who was the Director General for Schools as it was called. We had to bring him in very quickly as well. He then subsequently became the Permanent Secretary at Education and then at the Home Office and is now heading the Public Appointments Commission. So we had extremely well versed, experienced people who were committed to the agenda of raising standards and of improvement which was the mantra.

So the days were filled with enthusing, motivating, informing those around us who were crucial to doing the job of taking forward in Parliament. Including winning over Labour Members of Parliament who were, at the time, still sceptical of our radical approach and the push we were making to improve standards, that we were in the right direction and we were serious and we were going to do the job.

Willis: You mention some things that we'll be dealing with later in the conversation. You referred to the Standards and Effectiveness Unit set up in 1997, to what extent was that a message to the civil servants that you meant business and were resistant to the traditional conservative element in Whitehall?

Blunkett: It was a message that we wanted people who were hands on, experienced and prepared to look outwards as well as inwards. It was not an objectionable message because we said to people please join us. If you've got a commitment, an interest, not only will we include you in the purposeful endeavour from the

Department but we'll second you outwards as well so you can get experience. So we wanted people both coming in and experiencing life outside the Department.

We got a very good response from people who, with the best will in the world had seen a Government whose time had run out, whose energy had run out. Therefore were looking for that kind of enthusiasm and infusion of energy and drive and above all clarity of purpose and direction. So we received a good response to that. It was also a message to the education world outside, that we wanted people in the Department who knew what they were talking about in order to be able to match and to take on those forces outside who always were able to say, well you as politicians don't know really what you're talking about, the Department's out of touch, we're the ones who know and we don't like what you're saying.

So we wanted to actually say, I'm afraid we do know what we're talking about. We do have people who are hands on, on very practical and when you throw objections we'll be able to deal with those objections, or we'll have people who will hear them and be able to reflect those into us, into the policy process and say, yes these are valid criticisms or valid concerns. Let's have a look at practical ways of dealing with them.

Willis: It's interesting to know about the role of the Standards and Effectiveness Unit set up in 1997. Can you describe the means you were able to employ to win over the Department and how effective were statements such as The Prime Minister will support me or I have the Prime Minister's support?

Blunkett: Well there were three elements. Firstly the credibility of Professor Sir Michael Barber in his role as leading the unit and recruiting people. Secondly the enormous support and commitment of Michael Bichard who understood that his role was to ensure that policy was both appreciated, well informed, and was then clearly implemented, and thirdly that the Prime Minister was wholly behind radical progressive improvement and change. So the Prime Minister's reform agenda was central to the Government and that education was central to the Government's reforms. So it was a two-way process.

The Prime Minister had decided that alongside economic recovery and employment issues that I was also dealing with, the reform of education and putting education at the centre of Government policy was a pre-requisite to persuading people that this Government was committed and clear about its objectives. That was a terrific boon to me so educate the – the mantra that education, education, education was central to Government success, enabled me to persuade the Department and of course all the hands-on players outside.

The school heads, teachers in the classroom, academics in teacher training that we – and of course the teacher unions – that we were serious and that we have the backing from No. 10 Downing Street to make it possible.

Willis: Can we please talk about the more general question about the way in which the Civil Service machine presented counter-objectives to you as a Minister and there is a popular assumption reinforced by TV programmes such as Yes Prime Minister about bureaucratic obstructionism. How far did the civil servants obstruct your policies and can you give an example of how you managed to overcome the wishes of civil servants who opposed your policies?

Blunkett: I think the most obvious and immediate reflection was the Secretary to the Cabinet and Head of the Civil Service which at that point was a joint role, Robin now Lord Butler, who was an extraordinarily able professional mandarin. Someone who'd had a lifetime's experience in the Civil Service and was deeply suspicious of us bringing in Michael Barber and immediately infusing the Department with outsiders. This was something that in his own experience and in having defended the Civil Service against a whole range of assaults over many years, found very difficult to take.

Had the Prime Minister and the Permanent Secretary at the Department not wholly backed that initial move within the first few days of the new Government, then the Standards and Effectiveness Unit would have died at birth. So that was the first example. The second was really ensuring that with the support of the Leadership Team in the Department, that's the official Leadership Team, that there was an understanding with my own special advisors and with the Education Ministerial Team that we were able to have robust conversations and form a common front.

So that we set up – before it became fashionable – a joint board between the permanent officials and the Ministers and my special advisors so that we were meeting in common. We were determining the direction and thrashing out where policy was immediately feasible and where we needed to do more work. That was then transmitted both in terms of the message that the joint board sent, and the fact that it had the backing of all the players involved out to the Department. We also held departmental meetings right across the country, not just in the London based department but also in the outside offices, including my own City of Sheffield where the Department had a very big operation.

Holding meetings of the civil servants and speaking to them, presenting to them where we were going, what our policies were about, and then taking questions and asking them. Also as e-mail gradually developed, it was in its very early stages, initially it was telephone conference facilities and faxing and then we got onto e-mail at the very end of my four years in the Department, to be able to get people to be interactive and to feel that they were part of the process. We didn't do enough of it but it was ground breaking at the time. If I had my time again I'd have done even more of it.

Willis: So would you say that the expertise of the civil servants could be explained more in terms them being truly experts rather than amateurs?

Blunkett: Well it was to get them to feel that having some expertise and being able to use it would be valued in terms of their promotion prospects. The problem with the Civil Service more broadly – and it certainly was just as true of the Department for Education and Employment – was that people felt that their prospects for promotion and elevation would be in moving quickly between jobs, demonstrating a breadth of experience rather than a breadth of knowledge about a particular area and the ability to implement and see through policy.

We made some significant progress in the Department but it was against the backcloth of the Civil Service Commission and the way in which the Civil Service across Government worked. Being inimical to that, in other words we were pushing water uphill at the time in terms of saying, we don't want every job to have to be contestable. We want to be able to add to people's job portfolio and promote them within the job without being accused of breaking internal equality rules, which had become a burden rather than a liberator.

In terms of – for instance the Bill Team as they're called, the Team where they come together to develop the legislation, to incorporate the policy, to make sure that the legal drafting would be watertight and to assist Ministers both in the Commons and the Lords in carrying through that legislation. The classic formula was then for the Team to be disbanded whereas my idea was that they'd developed the expertise, the knowledge about what was required, why not use that expertise in terms of enabling them to become part of the delivery mechanism. That wasn't common and we only managed it once whereas actually it should have been the common practise.

Willis: In you book The Blunkett Tapes you write that it is important to understand about the power of the Treasury. Could you kindly elaborate on this view and how hard for example was it to get Gordon Brown to allocate funds for the Class Size Pledge?

Blunkett: Well it was very difficult dealing with the Treasury because of the power structures within Government. I mean I was very fortunate that I had the backing of the Prime Minister and that on the Employment part of my brief, and therefore the skills element, Gordon Brown in terms of implementing his wider economic policies needed at least some modest buy-in from me. Therefore the quid pro quo of his buy-in to what we were doing. So we were fortunate that the triangle allowed us that kind of influence and in some cases the political clout, the power, to be able to deal with the Treasury.

I say that because the Treasury obviously have the power of the purse strings and that should never be underestimated. But they also have the power, as we developed Service Level Agreements, to be able to block or to seek to influence the way in which policy developed on the back of resourcing. As it happened, there were areas where Gordon Brown and I had common agreement. Early years he was at least in theory committed to – although he was more inter-ested in child care than he was in the Sure Start and Child Development Policies.

Education Maintenance Allowances – which I was very keen on – would not have happened had he not realised that the commitment to getting young people to stay on in post-16 education was absolutely crucial to his own commitment to developing skills as part of growth and a modern global economy. So there was a synergy there that worked very well. However, it had to be underpinned by hard headed bruiser politics which meant taking Gordon on when it was necessary and riding with his interests when it was appropriate.

I think we managed to do that, particularly in the Education and Employment Brief because we had the employment, the skills and the higher education brief and early years all in the same programme. That meant that there was a genuine cross departmental interest between the Treasury and the Department for Education and Employment. Sometimes we clashed. He didn't like me intervening and being involved with the Monetary Policy Committee of the Bank of England – which I thought was essential to the Employment and Skills Brief – and was very upset when we took a line on that aspect of economic policy that influenced interest rates and Bank of England policy. Those areas we did clash on.

Willis: Obviously it was quite hard to win over the Treasury to your cause at times and I know you were noted for standing up to the Treasury and civil servants, but turning more towards the limitations you experienced on policy making when you were Secretary of State for Education, to what extent did the Prime Minister's Special Advisors and the Chief Executive of Schools, then Chris Woodhead, thwart your policies on education?

Blunkett: Well let's take the issue of Downing Street first. I think it has to be remembered, although not everyone – including those involved – actually do remember this, that Andrew Adonis didn't come into Downing Street until 15 months after the General Election. By that time we'd developed substantial elements of the policy, both from what the work we'd done in opposition and the immediate expansion of that work in Government. I had a Special Advisor, Conor Ryan who subsequently went to work for Tony Blair, who understood the workings of Downing Street and was very empathetic to Andrew Adonis when he did enter Downing Street.

So we were able to do more business than would otherwise have been possible because of the relationship that they developed. Anyone who works for a Prime Minister has a lot of time on their hands. They don't have to do the day-to-day development work, they don't have to do the Parliamentary activity. They don't have to win people over. They can visit, they can speak at conferences, they can listen to people whispering in their ear. So they have more time on their hands to develop ideas. I had to come to terms with the fact that that was a positive gain because you were – you always needed to know what the next step would be.

It would be when you've taken the first two steps and if you were going to continue reform and improvement you hadn't completed it when you'd carried through the first tranche. So I had to learn that. Andrew Adonis had to learn that there were practical issues at stake as well as broader policy and political implications. It was more difficult with Chris Woodhead. Chris had been given a fairly wide brief by the previous Secretary of State, partly because the Government under John Major had run out of steam, partly because John Major had asked Gillian Shepherd, the previous Secretary of State, to keep a fairly low profile.

They'd had a fairly rough time under Chris Patten and that I think was unfortunate for Gillian because I liked her and I thought she could have done a great deal more. Anyway, the upshot was that Chris Woodhead had been given a fairly free hand was well liked by the right-wing media and had a very, very high profile. I didn't mind Chris Woodhead throwing up ideas if he was prepared to actually understand that all ideas have to be part of a synergy. They have to be part of a dialogue, a Socratic dialogue. I used to try and explain to him – meant that there were always two sides to an argument.

I agreed with him or he agreed with me on about 95 per cent of the issues that we debated. It was just that Chris could never understand that sometimes you have to compromise and if I didn't agree with him on the five per cent, I was the Secretary of State and my policy would prevail. That led to a very, very difficult and robust – sometimes constructive, sometimes destructive relationship. The same applied to Professor Sir Michael Barber who understood entirely where Chris Woodhead was coming from and the reform agenda but also understood what was possible and feasible.

For instance, Chris's policy on a particular form of synthetic phonics was understood very well by us but seemed to us to be entirely contradictory to his belief that schools should be left alone to determine their own curriculum, their own schemes of work and their own education policy. Well you can have one but you can't have the other. You could have a reading list which determined a particular type of literature for schools to follow, but you couldn't then say that the schools were entirely free to develop their own literature within the English Curriculum. So there were enormous contradictions in the ideological thrust of Chris Woodhead that we used to have to point out to him.

Willis: What observations can you make please about the relationship between the Education Department and the Local Authorities? Did they, for example, have any effect on influencing the policies you were seeking to introduce?

Blunkett: Well we'd made it clear so that the Local Authorities were under no misapprehension that the only thing that we wanted them to really put at the centre of their policy was raising standards. We'd said that it was standards not structures. We'd said we'd try and heal the breach between those who wanted grant maintained and those who were committed to community schools. We developed the foundation school concept and of course eventually, before I left the Department, we put in to place the proposals for Academy Schools.

Based on the collaborative, mutual approach where schools would help schools, where there would be outreach into the wider community, recognising the school community and not just the school as a factory to put children through a particular process. The Local Authorities were highly suspicious of what we were doing because it did involve acknowledging what had been put in place by Ken Baker in the '88 changes, 1988 changes, with Local Management Schools. Namely, that schools run schools, that the head of the school, the school leadership team had to take responsibility and be accountable for what went on in their school with the support of, rather than the control of, the Local Authority.

We were still coming – I think Local Authorities were still coming to terms with that. I gave Estelle Morris – who at the time was my number two, she followed Stephen Byers as the Minister of State responsible – a very clear remit and total backing in dealing with Local Authority failure, hence the actions that were taken in Hackney, in Leeds, in Liverpool and of course in Islington. So actions were taken where Local Authorities were clearly failing to give the necessary drive and support for the changes that we required. I think she was extremely effective in doing that.

Willis: How were your policies affected by the press? Did they cause you to revise or amend any policies that you were trying to push through?

Blunkett: I think that the press in one sense were a driver for the kind of changes that we were bringing about, albeit that many of those writing had little experience of state education. Their own experience and their children's experience tended to be in the private sector. I don't think that this was a great disadvantage to us in the sense that being driven to more radical approaches on the lines that you've already laid out is a positive not a negative. Had the education policy been buffeted from pillar to post by columnists or campaigners within the press then I would have been more concerned about it.

I think the only thing that could be said about the press was that, the right wing press in particular were obsessed with whether Chris Woodhead's [scriptures] were being taken seriously and the more left of centre press were obsessed with getting rid of Chris Woodhead. I have to say to people, I'm sorry but we're not obsessed with Chris Woodhead. So we had to sort of make sure that in dealing with the commentary that we were receiving in the media, we weren't diverted into the interests and the direction of one individual, powerful as he was, because he was running Ofsted.

Willis: To what extent did the teaching unions constrain your policies? For example with regard to the General Teaching Council, did they strangle any attempts to have a worthy GTC by demanding to have reserve seats on its Council?

Blunkett: Well I think that the Trade Unions had got the message long before the General Election, not least in their relationship with me, and understood where we were coming from. I think that they misunderstood our efforts to set up a General Teaching Council and because they weren't wholeheartedly in favour of it, and failed to understand the role it could play, they did play a part in at least partial strangulation which led it to be less successful, subsequently hard to defend.

I've always been a believer that something that is rooted and has widespread support is much more difficult to abolish than something that has been undermined from the beginning. It was a shame because the GTC could have played a much bigger part in professional development and the standing of the teaching profession. In a sense we have to work round that with the College of School Leadership with Teach First and developments that were after my time like Teaching Schools Alliance and activities of that sort which could have been underpinned and supported by a very powerful GTC.

Willis: How important is the personality of the Minister in getting policies accepted would you say?

Blunkett: Oh I think that having a strong, determined and very clear Secretary of State and a group of like-minded ministers makes a very big difference. It is the team, not just the Secretary of State. I mean I was fortunate to go to negotiate – not universally – but pretty much with the Prime Minister teams in the four years I was there, that were really committed both personally to me but more importantly to the policy and the reform agenda. There were hiccups where Gordon Brown, with the powerful relationship he had with the Prime Minister was able to ask for a particular post, but compared with other front bench ministerial teams pretty much the teams that I wanted.

That was a great advantage because working as a team, being able to give individuals their head, meant that the team succeeded and not just the Secretary of State. I was taught this when in opposition, when someone who eventually went back to New Zealand to become a Vice Chancellor of the University, Bryan Gould, showed me years before that the success of the team is beneficial to the leader of that team as well as to the individuals. If you can back, support, allow individuals to flourish you get something out of it, the team undoubtedly get something out of it and therefore the Government in terms of implementing policy gets something out it. I think that's a lesson that is often forgotten.

Willis: What was your position in regard to Brussels in Europe? Did they try and interfere with your policies or help you to promote them?

Blunkett: No I – on the employment side we were trying to drive more radical change as with the Lisbon Treaty in 2000 in terms of trying to free up the labour market and have much more radical approaches to employment policy. On the education front there was absolutely no influence whatsoever other than taking a greater interest ourselves in what was working in Europe and the world. So Michael Barber was particularly interested in this and in the PISA process in terms of higher education.

Baroness Tessa Blackstone, I asked to take a particular interest in that European dimension of trying to develop at least some understandable policies that allowed transferability, teachers including higher education to be able to move more easily between institutions and to have a greater connectivity with Europe. Apart from that the European Union itself and the Commission had very little influence over our policies.

Willis: Would you say the influence they had was quite positive? I'm thinking of the grant of £160 million as part of Objective Four of the European Union Funding?

Blunkett: Yes we were very keen on the skills side to develop both the European Social Fund and Objective Four. With higher education the Bologna discussions about again recognition and connectivity that – I mean it sounds a small amount of money now from Objective Four but it was important at the time. You mentioned the issue of negotiations with the Treasury over class sizes. We'd had to scrape together from the abolition of vouchers for private education, we'd had to scrape very small amounts of money and make them go a very long way.

It was almost like the feeding of the 5,000. That was true of European Social Fund and Objective Four money as well. So we were taking hold of very small amounts of money, trying to match them to existing funds, trying to get some momentum and proving what worked in order to be able to then go into comprehensive spending reviews. For instance in 2000 with a much clearer perspective of what – where the money should go and how it would be beneficial to invest in particular areas.

Willis: I did have two final questions David, looking at the contemporary scene, can you give a viewpoint on how you would describe Michael Gove's style of leadership and approach to policy making?

Blunkett: I think it has a combination of being driven by West London dinner party conversations about what worked in private education in the Home Counties in the 1950s and a genuine desire to improve standards. Although Michael Gove is a zealot and is extremely difficult to read and understand, I do believe that his willingness to alter his policies a little in relation to the way he's approached the curriculum, the way he's approached the judgement on standards in education and what was originally the EBacc and his obsession, ideological obsession, with free schools is underpinned by a genuine desire to improve standards.

I think the difficulty is that the policies become increasingly contradictory. It's hard to believe that improved standards in the classroom which is at the very heart of any improvement in education, can be validated by believing that you could have untrained teachers in the classroom as opposed to teaching in a system, some instructors under the direction of professionally trained teachers. It's hard to believe that you can believe that there should be programmes of study and a curriculum if you then say that the heart of your policy is free schools which don't have to follow in any sense those strictures.

It's hard to believe that you want extraordinarily good world class leadership if you're able to bring people in as school leaders who've got no experience of school leadership.

Willis: If I can end by asking you a question on the philosophies of education which I think is appropriate in view of your knowledge of political science and your education at university. How much were your views of education influenced by the philosophy of education and what are your thoughts, for example, on Jean-Jacques Rousseau's theory of the general will whereby society ought to always act for the common good and Adam Smith's perspective that in the economy, everyone should be self-interested. So by default not necessarily acting for the common good?

Blunkett: Well this touches on my interests more broadly in political philosophy. I mean I was very fortunate to have three years at university when I could read and think and have that kind of dialogue. It wasn't the degree I got at the end of it but that opportunity to at least to have examined the competing philosophical theories and their application in the modern era. That led me to believe that the common good can be underpinned by enlightened self-interest.

That we need therefore, to be able to persuade people who want the right thing for their child and instinctively will take the actions necessary to achieve that. That it will only work for them, their family and the subsequent wellbeing of their child if others around them are equally well educated and the outcomes lead to a society in which their child will be able to flourish, both economically and in terms of social and cultural life. So that a well-educated child in a vacuum which results in them having to put barbed wire around enclaves in which they live, in a society that's disintegrating and an economy that can't compete, will not be of benefit to anyone.

Now that is quite a hard ask but it has to be underpinned by persuading people in the political arena more generally that they are voting both for their own interests but for the wider good of society. Therefore there is a community and society interest which is why schools have to be at the heart of their community, that when you encourage and incentivise them to do well for their pupils, they should be prepared to share that experience and that wellbeing, both with others schools and in outreach to parents and the community they serve. So it has a moral imperative to it as well as a drive for standards for individual children.

Willis: Thank you, if we could possibly close the interview at this point. Your answers to the questions have been really fascinating and I really do thank you.

Blunkett: Okay I could just say this, that the advantage that Crosland – I know that Roy Jenkins didn't really want to be Education Secretary – but Crosland and others didn't have, which was that at the time I had a department which was so extensive that it could play a much bigger role within the Government and governance of the country. In other words it had the wider resource base, it had the clout in dealing with both Prime Minister and Chancellor and it had a longitudinal synergy which regrettably the balkanisation of Government which subsequently took place, didn't have.

I don't think it can be underestimated that having that political clout as well as having the backing of the Prime Minister from the beginning made an enormous difference.

Willis: I intend to prepare a transcript of our conversation and to let you have a copy for you to amend and revise.

Blunkett: That would be fine.

Willis: Well, David Blunkett thanks very much indeed.

Blunkett: You're very welcome, good luck with it.

Willis: Thank you very much, all the very best.

Blunkett: Thank you Richard, bye-bye.

Willis: Bye-bye.

The Rt Hon. Kenneth, Lord Baker, CH

[Aside discussion]

Willis: Good morning. Thanks very much for agreeing to talk to me this morning, Lord Baker. I feel very honoured. This conversation is being recorded. The time and date are 10:30 a.m. on 17 October 2013. As I mentioned before when I wrote to you in July and August of this year, the aim of the work is to model it along the lines of the book, *The Politics of Education*, which Maurice Kogan wrote. It was published by Penguin in 1971. The chat in short is intended to analyse the role of Education Minister and to see how your experiences in government sheds light on this role.

Some of the answers to these questions may appear in existing publications. My aim here is to stick to Kogan's format, so quite clearly other sources may contain the answers. It's my intention to have a complete record for the purposes of the book I intend to write and to include the transcript hopefully of our conversation this morning. So is it okay to kick off?

Baker: Okay, right-o.

Willis: What would you say draws men and women, do you think, to the often precarious and dicey career of the politician?

Baker: Well, I think that – and certainly it happened to me during my education process. You got involved with wider, more public affairs and public issues. I also remember my history tutor – and that's the history teacher at St Paul's – when we were 14 and there was some great crisis in Australia and New Zealand in the 1950s. [It was enormous]. He said, how much do you know all about this? The class was barely following this. So he then had a sloping desk in the classroom provided us with the daily papers. He said, you should have views on all of these things. That was one of the reasons, one of the [unclear] on which I was aware of wider issues in the world.

My family was fairly interested. My father was particularly interested in global events and politics, what was happening [unclear] at home. So I suppose really one would say that it's an interest in the wider area of public affairs that really is the beginning of politicians.

Willis: What other careers apart from politics did you consider?

Baker: Well, when I left Oxford, I didn't know what to do. My [family was a] civil servant – I didn't want to be a civil servant and so I joined Shell. That was the thing, because they paid the most money in those days – the princely salary of £750. I worked there for a year really on the economics of the oil industry. I didn't like that and so I then applied for a job elsewhere and became the chairman of a company in the clothing industry. I realised that I wanted to do something different and from that developed a career in business.

I was [religious in things] I was asked to do in this particular business. It was a dreadful warehouse in central London that got totally out of control. The goods in and goods out wasn't properly controlled and the stock rooms were – and I was given the task of pulling it around in three months, which I enjoyed enormously. I got the [unclear] there for running businesses.

I then moved on from there to a very . . . trust and he invested in businesses with the trust's money. He would then nurse them back or expand them. I was made by him the chief executive of business that was going bust, it was [like] Marks & Spencer. This is in the early '60s now. We're talking about the '60s. I was given the job of chief exec to pull it round. I, after two years, did pull it around and made it profitable.

That is a very unusual career for a politician these days. I had to make a choice in 1968. At the same time, I was interested in politics. From '64, I thought – because in those days, if you wanted to get in the House of Commons, you had first to fight for a safe Labour seat, then a marginal, then you might get a safe, because I fought a safe Labour seat against [Ian McCarter] in 1964. In '66, I was given the chance of a marginal at . . . at Acton, but I stayed on being a candidate.

In 1968, the Member of Parliament for Acton, Bernard Floud, committed suicide. He shouldn't really have been a politician . . . university really. He was quite wealthy. All the rumours and his wife dying from . . . committed suicide. There was going to be a by-election. I was bound to win the by-election as a candidate. Wilson was massively unpopular . . . and so I had to decide whether I should stay in this business I was in or whether I should go and stand as a candidate and clearly win. It was a very difficult decision. I . . . politics. He said, look . . . you can go on being the director of this company until we find a substitute. Obviously I couldn't go on as a full-time chief executive. That was . . . and so I made that choice.

Now today I don't think anybody would make that choice, the same choice I made about business, because life in politics has become much less attractive. It's much more . . . It's much more constituency . . . than it was in my time. You're absolutely [discouraged]. If you get into the [stage] very closely, we've also almost been forbidden as a Member of Parliament to bring any active interests outside of being a Member of Parliament. So I think anybody today would not have accepted that or made that decision, but I did make that decision. I saw that I was elected and that really took me to politics . . . when we weren't in office . . . and I went back into business . . . career path . . . for a politician.

Willis: Would you say your choice of career then was determined by family and social background?

Baker: Not entirely. My father wanted me – coming from a civil service background – to be a civil servant. I did not find that at all attractive. I made it clear to him actually. I think he was a little upset to some extent and a bit surprised I entered politics. He considered it to be a very uncertain career, but I think I made the right choice. I don't think it was really affected really by my family background at all.

Willis: Now if we turn towards the post of Education

Secretary, could you let me know a typical day in your life as Education Secretary?

Baker: Let you know about what, did you say?

Willis: A typical day in your life as Education Secretary.

Baker: My time in the office was usually before nine o'clock – maybe 8:30 – so my office was within the Department of Education . . . the day. When I was appointed by Margaret Thatcher in 1986 – so she obviously called me in and said, would you be Education Secretary – and I was expecting to be told by her what she wanted done. That was not the case. She said, look, the only problem – the big problem at that time was the strike . . . 18 months. Keith Joseph and Chris Patten had not been able to solve it. She said, we must really try to look for a solution to this major problem facing the Education Secretary. But she said, look, go away and come back to me in two months and tell me what your ideas are in education, which surprised me – I may say a very pleasant surprise.

So that's what I did. For the next four, six weeks, I fashioned then the ideas and policies which led to the . . . Reform Act of 1988. I went back and talked to her. I did tell her in my official meeting that I was very keen to establish a type of technical college and make that [unclear] independent of local authorities . . . She did not tell me what she wanted to be done and so I [was given] a free hand. Having been a Member of Parliament, of course, one knows a lot about the education in one's constituency. I repre-sented Marylebone and . . . I had in my constituency one of the best schools . . . grammar school . . . by Shirley Williams actually . . . and very deceitful actu-ally, the way it was done.

I therefore came with a certain package as it were of what I wanted to see. I also sought a very broad course in policy, so I had some very strong views of my own . . . When I got to the parliament, I found there was some work to be done . . . but not very much actually. There was . . . in charge of it. I said, well, we really must find a way of trying to pull it all together nationally . . . National Curriculum and . . . very much work to be done on that . . . I had my own views of schools.

Also, there aren't many . . . I was very keen to support the . . . to devolve budgets from the local authorities to schools and . . . very clear that they were very successful . . . and so my group of officials, that was one of the first things we decided to do and to extend that on a much wider basis where many local authorities objected [unclear] and that sort of thing. Transferring control of budgets to the actual schools is probably one of the most significant changes I made.

Willis: I think you've touched upon some of the things that we're going to mention later on in the conversation, but could you tell me, please, how heavy the responsibilities of being Education Secretary weighed on you?

Baker: I was immensely proud and flattered to be offered the post, because we had not made very much progress from 1981 to '86 in transforming the education system. Although Keith had lots of very interesting ideas, he was not a very effective sort of minister. He had some very distinguished and clever civil servants who I think seduced him into very theoretical arguments about the nature of education, which he found very fascinating. There was a group of very good civil servants . . . was one and he was the one, I think, who seduced Keith intellectually, as it were, into exploring very interesting avenues of theoretical approaches to education.

There was a good [unclear] and there were two other senior officials. I started talking to them as a group immediately, because I knew I wanted to change things and I wanted to have the department with me. I also had an exceptional permanent secretary [who's just died]. He realised there's a lot that had to be done and changed and we could not go on as we were, because there was a huge amount of criticism [unclear] education system . . . where he dared to tread into the holy ground of political [masochism]. He was virtually seen off last year . . . and very little . . . in that speech . . . and quite frankly . . .

Willis: In the date of more consensual politics, Anthony Crosland considered it took about two years to get full control over policy making in the department. Were you able to have a strong influence once you were in office bearing in mind you had a strong mandate from the electorate to govern?

Baker: Well, yes, the need to improve the education system at that stage had become compelling. There was a huge criticism from industry that we were producing youngsters that they didn't want to employ and a lot of criticism all the time on that score. So something had to be done. That was one of the strengths that I had that I was the person who was going to have a chance to do it. That was really very important.

I found it was possible to persuade civil servants of the necessity of change, to discuss things around the table. I said to them [unclear] you bring one of your under-secretaries or your assistant secretaries with you, because I want to hear their views as well. That was a really rather exceptional and extraordinary request which they didn't embrace with enthusiasm at the beginning. So I extended the basis of negotiation much further down into the department.

Willis: Could you comment more about the expertise of the civil servants? Did you find them amateurs or were they truly experts?

Baker: No, the civil servants I had were great experts on the education system of our country. There was no doubt about that at all and particularly during a period of time where there was a considerable degree of control from the centre. The Education Department really did control the education system of the country in a very detailed way. Although local authorities provided it, their control over local authorities was quite extensive actually. They would say the school had to have a certain number of school pupils, let us say [1200]. They would decide that not on the passive school . . . but in order to get the balance right locally . . .

There were lots of decisions like that that were going on all the time in the department. I also found that the unions came in constantly to talk to ministers. They had separate rooms for them to talk [unclear] on the department and I . . . that's not their job. They have a job to represent their members and it's come in and talk to us about issues. I was not anti-union at all. It seemed to me that the whole arrangement was not right in the education world. So I would say to the civil servants I had, we're talented people and very scrupulous people. When they realised that I wanted on behalf of the government to change things, they supported me very strongly.

Willis: On that note, can we just discuss a bit more about the more general question about the way in which the civil service machine presented counter-objectives to you as minister? There is a popular assumption reinforced by TV programs – such as Yes, Prime Minister – about bureaucratic obstructionism. How far did the civil service obstruct your policies and can you give examples of how you managed to overcome the wishes of civil servants who opposed your policies?

Baker: I did not have that trouble with my civil servants. The civil servants I had, I didn't feel at any time I was being positively stopped by what they would do. They were not trying to stop me. They would present to me arguments for and against obviously changes. Take the question of school number. There was quite a long debate on that [unclear] defending the school number, because that was [the central planning] too. But when they saw that I was prepared to remove it or . . . it, they began to change their views and said, well, if you want to do it, then may we suggest that this is a possible way of doing it? So like all civil servants, when they see that there is movement going along, they will respond to it. They did not at any time simply frustrate what I was doing.

Willis: If you were challenged in any way, what means did you employ to win over the [DES]? Did you resort to statements such as the prime minister will support me or I will have the prime minister's support?

Baker: No, they knew I had that. I didn't have to say that. Well, because I had the support of Margaret Thatcher and they knew that Margaret Thatcher was so dissatisfied with the education system. She was quite reluctant ever to speak about her own time as Education Secretary. I think she was a bit hurt by it actually, because she signed up for it and [unclear] was the only other [minister]. I think she rather . . . No, they knew that I'd been put there to change things, so they did not seek to obstruct what I was doing. I took great pains to win over them and tried to convince them intellectually that what we were proposing was right and would produce good results.

Willis: Can you summarise in more detail the main roles that the department ought to be exercising in relation to policy and what should the role of the department be in as far as you think it should be?

Baker: Say that again.

Willis: Yes, can you give an outline of the main roles that the department should be exercising in relation to policy? What should the role of the department be in as far as you think it should be?

Baker: Well, the role of the department is really to administer the area for which they're responsible. They're responsible for the education system of our country. I have a very wide portfolio. I'm not sure about subsequent ministers. I was responsible for the school system, the . . . universities and the science budget, so I had a variety of experts in each of those areas. I had great respect for the civil servants in them. Every minister has to deal with a series of immediate problems . . . and there were about six or seven. This is all in my book by the way, The Turbulent Years.

There were a series of burning fires that I had to put out, like the [unclear] books in primary school, problems with the funding of [FE] colleges. You have to deal with that. For that, you do depend upon the advice of the civil servants for your strategy. They were also good at that. Certainly I found that the whole philosophy of the Department of Education – the whole attitude – was very deeply ingrained with the education establishment as well. Many of the civil servants' wives were teachers or married into the teaching profession or at universities involved in the education world.

There was a whole world of education departments that was very closely involved with the Department of

Education. It was – what was the phrase now? The education establishment was another much more difficult body to deal with – very, very reluctant to . . . changes to education – very, very reluctant indeed, always looking upon anything which dared to challenge . . . principals as basically unsound and dangerous and so that the bigger problem was not so much the civil servants in my department but the education establishment into which, of course, the [teaching unions were] closely involved.

Willis: You mentioned when Margaret Thatcher was education minister, she regretted the number of orders she had – in signing orders to abolish grammar schools, so she felt she had been taken in by the DES. Can you say a little more about how the DES opposed your policies or are you saying that there was very little opposition to your policies?

Baker: I have to say to you they did not seek to oppose my policies. When we established the [bones] of the National Curriculum, that was . . . I knew some of the things that had to be done . . . do it and so they came up with the proposal and the team of people that would do . . . to establish a National Curriculum and then we set up a series of working groups in each of the areas to establish the actual contents of the curriculum. All those working groups had to get a balance of interests. You had to get the right-wing [mathematicians to the left-wing mathematicians] if you like, to put it very crudely.

I know in English it was very fascinating . . . National Curriculum, so I said, well . . . report basically . . . on the state of English education. They came up with the most appallingly inadequate set of proposals. They were not strict on grammar or spelling. So I had to get another group to do that [edified] by the chance that this review was going to be [better]. He therefore produced a result which I knew was immediate, a much more rigorous approach to English education.

So the civil servants in all of that were very good. When they knew the National Curriculum was to be included in legislation, I had to prepare the bill setting out all these ideas. They wanted the ideas to succeed. They knew that I had influence at Whitehall and all civil servants like a minister who has high profile and wins Whitehall debates. They also knew that I could persuade the prime minister to do it . . . what I was doing of more independent schools, a National Curriculum with increased rigour, tests and details. Margaret liked those. When they knew that the prime minister liked them, this was not just a strange minister, fly-by-night coming in and breaking out his own prejudices, they backed it and gave a very good service.

Willis: Both Sir Keith Joseph and Margaret Thatcher considered that the DES was "an awful department". Would you agree then that you had a better experience at the DES?

Baker: I had a much better experience at the DES. I don't think it was an [awful] department. I think that it was a very traditional department. I think it was far too close to the educational establishment and influenced by it, but one has to shake that up. So we gave it a good shake and shake it up. [That day], they implemented my proposals which were the most fundamental changes in English education since 1946. Without their thoroughness and without their support, I'd never have been able to do what I did.

Willis: Thank you. When you were elected in May 1986, you clearly had several priorities. For example, you wanted to raise more money for education and you wanted to bring in fundamental reforms of the educational system. With regard to these areas, to what extent did the prime minister influence you to adopt these priorities? What other influences were at work in making you come to the conclusion that these were the priorities you wanted to take on board?

Baker: Well, one of the priorities, I did want to get more money for primary schools books. That was one of the big fires we had to put out and [unclear] more widely and more . . . at the end of the day. That was just one issue, but I would take the issues to her. I discussed them with her. She enjoyed those discussions. She realised she had a minister who was going to shake things up and in a way she failed [in shaking] up. What Margaret was lacking was a coherent flag emerging from the ministerial team at the Education Department to implement some of these things that she wanted to do.

Willis: Would you say there was harmony between what you wanted and what Margaret Thatcher wanted?

Baker: There was to some extent, but when you came to determining – first we introduced – if you look at the Tory manifesto in 1986, you will find there are nine pages of education changes and reforms. They would form the basis of the [British] Education Reform Bill.

There was everything. There was polytechnics coming out of the control of local authority, something interestingly which Keith Joseph had tried in 1981 and couldn't – at the end of the day, he had to abandon it. But I worked with one or two heads of polytechnics which were former Labour MPs and they [wanted to be] independent local authorities, because I got the rhythm going there. It was that. It was National Curriculum. It was league tables. It was [unclear] schools being elected to be independent, setting up some bright new fresh independent . . . technology colleges, delegated budgets in the school.

You've got all the elements that were in the 1986 political manifesto and then she tells me after winning the election to create a bill to introduce some of that legislation. [Some parties] virtually had to set up the curriculum groups . . . we – it was a very, very technical matter. When they saw that we were re-elected in [1986], the department threw – [its permanent] secretary threw its whole weight into making the changes successful.

The big dispute that one had was in the content of the National Curriculum, because I wanted a broad and balanced curriculum – maths, English, science and foreign languages and history . . . really down to – Margaret was much keener on maths, English and science. But I had to then produce to her papers on each subject and distinguishing between the foundation subjects and the other subjects and all the rest of it. She showed the committee [that did that] – the cabinet committee – and . . . so there was the liveliest debate almost I've ever attended. I argued very strongly. She argued back. Margaret didn't mind if you argued back some sense. If you were badly briefed and you argued sloppily, she'd absolutely crush you, but I was very well briefed.

I argued again and again in the national interest [unclear] there would be . . . truly excellent, but not at all. They had disputes as to whether – how tables should be used, whether children should know the tables by heart, at what age should you learn trigonometry. Each of these issues . . . supporting each one against the other. That did surprise me in maths. Science was less . . . and they just wanted about

[50/60] per cent of the curriculum. History, I knew was going to be highly controversial. English, I wasn't much settled on any set beliefs.

But those debates in the cabinet committee, it was blow for blow. She would go at me. I had . . . she would say, why . . . and I managed to handle her quite well. It was one of the incredible . . . of the cabinet – one of the meetings, I just – I'm not prepared to accept this at all, no. I was [reminded] about that by the . . . that he'd never seen before. She knew that she depended upon me to get this right, that it was an immensely complicated huge business to get all this through. We came eventually to agreement. The other matters, she swung . . .

Willis: Could you enlighten me on how strong you had to be to get the money you wanted for your reforms and perhaps outline your relationship with the treasury?

Baker: Well, the first big problem I had to try to resolve was the teacher's strike. This had been going on for 18 months. The teacher's negotiations, I mean . . . negotiations in those days . . . committee and the unions . . . It had been awful. Teachers were striking . . . so they had to have . . . and that was the first thing I had to resolve. I did manage eventually to persuade [Michael Dighton Lawson] to provide a reasonable offer – which they were not prepared to do – on the basis that the [bonus] system was completely abolished and the right to negotiate and their right to determine wages by the unions in the Education Department was removed completely.

What we did, we set up [an initial] advisory committee and they were given total budgets – several billion. They had to recommend how it should be awarded. That was one of the very successful things that I did in . . . negotiation. It was before the – because eventually it moved into the teacher's review body which just makes recommendations, but they actually had the money. They were told this is the package you've asked for – seven billion or something – and what do you recommend? They came up with some very [dangerous] suggestions.

One of the people I appointed to that commission was a very [ghastly] New Labour minister and an interesting person to talk to about . . . and they produced some of the best results for teachers in improvement of teacher's pay . . . were actually much better than bonuses. On that basis, the treasury was prepared to provide more money. So I think settling that [union] was correct . . . trade unions . . . which was rather radical. But it produced an effective system of reward for teachers, one of the best rewards they ever had actually and also an end to the strike.

Willis: What would you say – through the experience here – is the purpose of individual MPs in framing policies?

Baker: Well, the Select Committee on Education had been appointed by that time. It was to that committee that I announced one afternoon we were going to have a National Curriculum. I didn't go . . . Select Committee, because by that time we'd got the outlines of what we wanted to do. So I kept the MPs informed. Some MPs strongly in favour of what I was doing – mainly Conservative MPs, but some of them had been in support of their local authority . . . we don't need . . . education policy because we have Conservatives . . . good job . . . and so I had some MPs always who were reluctant to go along . . . that I wanted to go.

Whenever you try to reform something, you can't . . . Labour, of course, opposed it completely and said they'd reform everything and abolish everything once

in power. They didn't. They kept virtually everything I did in 1997 largely due to the influence of
David Blunkett. They did away with grant-maintained schools, but they reinvented them as trust
schools a few years later. So basically Labour
accepted everything we did eventually.

Willis: What observations did you make concerning the
relationship between the Education Department and
the local education authorities? I mean, did the
LEAs, for example, have any effect on influencing
your policies?

Baker: Well, some LEAs were very strongly opposed and
they lobbied their MPs to argue against them. There
were not in favour of grant-maintained schools.
They were not in favour of Technical Colleges
either. They weren't in favour of any – they . . .
because local authorities were very, very big educational powers. Many of them were exercising those
powers in a very inefficient and incompetent way.
Local education authorities did not mean good . . .
good management of education . . . not at all.

So there was a lot of opposition from them,
supported I may say by the education establishment
and universities. The education [unclear] were very
much in favour of the existing system and said, why
are you changing all this . . . and denied opportunities. To get my reforms through, it required first a
clear justification for reforms, well worked out
reforms and the support of the prime minister of the
day.

Willis: You've mentioned the role of the teaching unions.
How successful were they in blocking any of your
policies?

Baker: I don't think they were. They had such a bloody nose over the teacher's strike and they felt very excluded all the time. I did talk to them. I made it clear to them I would listen to them. If they had good ideas, I would consider them and implement any changes. If they don't . . . but the teachers knew everything about it and should never have their views challenged. They didn't want to have the parents being involved in at all. I said, well, forget it. I'm interested in what parents think. I was . . . over their heads. It was parents who wanted better education for their children. In many cases, parents were simply not getting it.

Willis: Well, quite clearly your policies were very significant. How did teachers welcome these policies and did they cause you to change direction on any of your decisions?

Baker: Of course, they commented on all the changes I made obviously. From time to time, I would see them. They would come in and they'd be very clear. There was a teacher's union called Professional Association of Teachers. I don't know whether it still exists.

Willis: They exist under another name, I believe.

Baker: Under another name, I think. They were the ones who were most supportive of what we were doing. They, for example, had never gone on strike. I think the big division about those unions that went on strike and those that didn't go on strike – there was quite a big division in all of that, but the education system was not going to be run by the teacher unions.

I think one of the most depressing things are their conferences at Easter when you get the [militants] on the television all over the Easter weekend giving the worst possible impression of the teaching profession of which I have a high regard. I come from a teaching family. My wife taught. My grandmother went to a teacher training college in Wandsworth in . . . I've still got the books with [her beautiful complicated handwriting]. I have several . . . who've been teachers. I have a high, high regard for the teaching profession.

Willis: Turning towards the [HMIs], did they contribute in any ways towards policy making?

Baker: Yes, [Amy Bolton] was the chief inspector and I have a high regard for. I'll tell you one thing . . . saying is that the individual reports that you get on schools, he says, do you read them right through, he said? Because that is [once] what you find out what's happening. The reports amounted to many pages. They're now about [two or three] pages long. I learnt a lot from them myself. You can see how thorough the inspection was and how big they were. I had a high regard for the inspections from the beginning. Amy Bolton was one of the senior . . .

Willis: Did organisations such as the [CBI] and individual employers have any say in affecting policies?

Baker: Well, to some extent they would acknowledge it in the background in that they were always complaining of how dreadful the system was. So therefore I was able to present a lot of what I did as changes for the better. That is what they liked. They'd also to turn the ship of education around and so it took a long time to implement all of the . . . I think. The things that were implemented at the end of my time were things like the delegated budgets, grant-maintained schools. It took some time to set up a framework and introduce the National Curriculum. At the same time . . . introduced GCSEs which was really . . . as well. But that was a series of bushfires, again, that had to be put out.

Willis: Did the press in any way cause you to modify any of your educational policies?

Baker: Yeah, I am told the press was very supportive of what I was doing Many of the press correspondents were people of quite high quality in my time. The editor for the TES was a very fine person. His name just escapes me, but he was brilliant at the time. It will come back in a moment. It's all in my book anyway.

Willis: Was it Stuart Maclure, was it?

Baker: John Clare was the – sorry?

Willis: Was it Stuart Maclure by any chance?

Baker: Who?

Willis: Stuart Maclure.

Baker: Stuart Maclure. I had a high regard for him. I spoke to him a lot. He was quite frank. He liked very much what I was doing. The bits [he] didn't like, he'd be very grumpy about. I didn't mind that at all. You get used to that in public life. But I respected him enormously. The education correspondent of The Telegraph, John Clare, was an outstanding figure – a figure respected in the education world. So was the education correspondent in The Guardian and in The Daily Mail. So I spoke to both a great deal, because I knew I had a persuading job to do. I was very frank with them. That, I think, paid off enormously because there was, at the end of the day, [clearly public] support for what I was doing.

Willis: It seems that policies can emerge in a variety of ways. Looking back at the National Curriculum and testing, what were the main influences here? Can you identify when the policy was . . . conceived? There must have been lots of forces at work, I would think. What do you think were the main ones?

Baker: Keith had done some work on curriculum reform, but it rather got bedded down. But I think there was a yearning in the department amongst professionals to move to form a National Curriculum on the very simple grounds that there should be uniformity of targets and curriculum across the country. So if somebody moved from Newcastle down to Plymouth, they'd move into a broadly similar education system that they left.

You must remember that in those days the only exam that existed in the education system – apart from 11-plus – was the GCSE at 16 and so schools had an enormous amount of discretion on their curriculum. Obviously what happened, good schools had good curriculums. Mediocre schools gave mediocre curriculums. Poor schools had poor curriculums. That was the pattern that the department had recognised and realised for a very long time, so there was a great degree of momentum behind the concept of a National Curriculum.

Willis: Sir Keith Joseph also advised you not to make the same mistake as he did when he attacked teachers. Can you expand upon your relationship with the teaching profession in the course of formulating, implementing policies?

Baker: I did not attack teachers. I reproached them for striking and I said that was wrong. I never tried to tell teachers how they should teach in the classroom. Coming from a teaching family, I knew that was impossible. That was for them to decide. But it was quite [unclear] for the government of the day to decide the content of what should be taught. Although teachers, some teachers – the [NUC] particularly and the other one, the [NSWT], were very strongly opposed. They were led by [a radical pretty left-wing] figure. Certainly . . . trade unions were very opposed to me . . . and all of that sort of thing. At Leicester University when I turned up, I was actually kicked to the ground on one occasion. [Unclear] universities.

In universities, I introduced student loans and also the cap to funding of students which were intended to be the paving stones to fees eventually. But I could not have got through Margaret Thatcher's government in those days fees without their saying so. So I think that was going to happen after me, but I set up the paving stones for it.

We also had trouble with university over the whole question of tenure, because there was some academic staff [unclear] teachers had been appointed in their 20s and had virtually done nothing either in teaching or in research for 20 or 30 years. They were just coasting along and . . . so we tackled the very vexed question of academic tenure. That was very difficult. We had to set up a special enquiry on the . . . the whole question of . . . but one did move towards slowly a proper contractual relationship between university staff and the universities – another area, of course, that was very controversial.

Willis: You spoke about the 1988 Education Reform Act. When did you realise with regard to that piece of legislation that you were passing a very radical law – something to compare with the 1944 Education Act?

Baker: I think one was aware of it from the very beginning and therefore we tried to get it as light as possible in a way it would survive. I therefore did realise that although the Labour party – very much guided by the unions – will oppose policy, I did lean over backwards to try and persuade them that some of the things I was doing were really sensible. On the whole, they eventually came around to a National Curriculum and tests. They didn't come around to . . . schools, but they realised that what I was doing was trying to implement what Jim Callaghan tried to do in 1976. So there was always an [undertone of] support for me in the Labour party which was very important.

But I was aware it was an important change, a very fundamental change. I wanted to introduce it in a way that it would succeed, so I actually decelerated some of the changes. I was urged by several MPs to immediately give all [private school heads] control of their budgets. I said, no, you've got to take this slowly. You've got to get . . . out, see what the problems are and then slowly extend it year by year by authority, authority, authority. Similarly with grant-maintained schools, there were some . . . let's get some going to show that they work properly and then you will get a movement going, which I think is a better way of doing it. So I was aware that it was quite significant.

Willis: Just two or three more questions to finish off with. Could you describe Michael Gove's style of leadership and approach to policy making?

Baker: Do I approve it, did you say?

Willis: No, can you describe it?

Baker: I don't think he's working as closely with the department as I was working with the department. I think a lot of his views come from his own personal attitudes as to what is needed in education. The department, I think, is struggling at times with them, but they're also trying to implement them too.

Willis: How much were your views of education influenced by the history and philosophy of education? I know you once heralded the Clarendon Commission reporting in Victorian England on the great public schools and its support for a common curriculum valuing breadth and balance. Did you draw some of your inspiration from such reports?

Baker: Yes, to some extent I did. I believe very strongly – to some extent I'm [unclear] in this in that if you want to change things, you should work on institutions and the reform of institutions and if necessary to create new institutions, like I did with . . . colleges, like I've done with University Technical Colleges, and announced this week career colleges.

I think if you want to reform something, you've got to do it in one of two ways. You either have a little experiment to see how it works and then go ahead, or have a very small experiment and then go ahead quite quickly. I believe the latter was the better way to do it – well, reasonably quickly – because if you just set up an experiment and you do it, it's exactly the same problem we have with University Technical Colleges.

When Ronald Dearing and I set this up five years ago, set up the concept, we commissioned research from Exeter University as to why we had failed in further education so badly for 150 years. It's a very interesting report. It was public, of course. The person at the end said – because at that time we'd got permission for two University Technical Colleges [unclear]. He said . . . them for five years, you won't be able to judge them for five years . . . four, five years or whether you try to create a movement. That was the moment that both Ron and I . . . was going to be a movement. We were so confident that our model was right, we said we would work more quickly than this, because otherwise nothing would happen for another 10 or 15 years.

Willis: If we could close the interview there, please. I intend to prepare a transcript of our chat and let you have a copy for you to amend and revise as you see fit.

Baker: Of course. It's a trip down memory lane for me.

Willis: Excellent. Well, Kenneth Baker, thanks very much indeed.

Baker: Of course, I made . . . local authorities again . . . That was a very important change. I was lucky in that there was a sense that the education system was failing the interests of the nation and something had to be done. The framework was there. There was a willing acceptance. My job was to make quite sure that what was done was going to be effective.

Willis: Excellent. Well, all the very best and thanks very much, Lord Baker.

Baker: Right-o, thank you very much.

Willis: Thank you. Bye-bye. Bye.